CHRISTOF WIECHERT

Teaching,
the Joy of Professio

An Invitation to
Enhance Your (Waldorf) Interest

CHRISTOF WIECHERT

Teaching,
the Joy of Profession

An Invitation to
Enhance Your (Waldorf) Interest

With drawings by Hans Dieter Appenrodt

VERLAG AM GOETHEANUM

The drawings in this book are from Hans Dieter Appenrodt who lives in the Netherlands. He created them in the last few years. They are finely crafted with deep psychological understanding and subtle humor. The precise expression in the lineal structure shows both lightness and meaningfulness. In these charming miniatures somewhat a kin to exercises I recognized what we strive for as valuable in education. I want to thank Hans Dieter Appenrodt for the permission to bring some of these drawings. The copyright is with the artist.

C. Wiechert

www.vamg.ch

Translated by Dorit Winter

1. edition 2012
2. edition 2015

Cover-Design by Wolfram Schildt, Berlin by using a drawing by Hans Dieter Appenrodt

Typesetting: Höpcke, Hamburg
Printing and binding: Druckhaus Nomos, Sinzheim
ISBN 978-3-7235-1473-3

CONTENT

PREFACE

Various fine publications have accompanied the rapid
spread of schools which arose from the educational
impulse and methods developed by Dr. Rudolf Steiner
(1861–1925), Austrian philosopher, scientist and educator. Especially since the second half of the 20th century
Waldorf Schools, sometimes also called Rudolf Steiner
Schools, invite people from all walks of life, from various religious and / or philosophical persuasions and from
every country and ethnicity to regard and to study the
child and the younger person as uniquely capable of development. Rudolf Steiner offered the basis for a practical understanding of this development as well as possibilities and levels of approach. In this new publication,
"Being a teacher: Do you like it?", the author opens up
vistas not only for parents but also for teachers, which
distinguishes this book as a unique contribution to exist-
ing literature in this field.

Christof Wiechert, a teacher with enormous experience resulting from many years in the classroom with
children at all age levels as well as carrying the responsibility as the leader of the Pedagogical Section at the
Goetheanum, Switzerland, shares valuable principles
of education with vivid examples which easily remain
with the reader to be called forth when a specific occasion arises. One of the outstanding qualities of the

book, which the author places at the very beginning, concerns the necessity of colleagueship among the teachers arising from mutual recognition and its subtle but persuasive effect on the pupils, the parents and the school community.

The importance which Christof Wiechert assigns to this aspect he sums up as: "Social life, getting along with each other, is a mighty task in school ... If you concern yourself energetically with recognition of the other, if you are willing to scrutinize your own actions, and if you make an effort to be awake to the ebb and flow of feelings that arise from your collegial dealings, you will have created a basis for inner autonomy."

An educational institution which can serve the needs of our time, namely helping children to develop their innate talents and placing seeds for the unfolding of new and necessary capacities, can arise only on this "basis for inner autonomy". Rudolf Steiner called the first school in Stuttgart, Germany, "Die Freie Waldorf-schule", "the Free Waldorf School" which in English does not convey the same meaning as in German. In the original wording it signifies free or independent from political (state), religious-confessional (church) and sociological (class-structure) constraints. For in such a setting the inner autonomy for the developmental stages of each child and also the individual and creative responsibility for the pedagogical unfoldment of the pupil on the part of the teacher can be promoted and safeguarded.

In some publications about Waldorf education one significant factor is missing – the parents. Here however, the author devotes direct emphasis to this indispensable reality: "One of the characteristics that makes a school into a Waldorf School is the intensive collaboration with the parents ... what is meant is the sort of working together which unites the parents and teachers for the sake of the children's welfare."

As a former Waldorf School teacher in California (Highland Hall Waldorf School) I look back now after many years have elapsed with deep gratitude to the inner and outer support which the parents offered to the process in which I was directly involved with *their* children. We enjoyed many happy (and a few challenging) moments together.

The far-reaching insights which Christof Wiechert describes in regard to the development of the child in relationship to the curriculum are too numerous to mention here. Also the same applies to the final chapter concerning "Inner Preparation or Self-Education" in which he addresses the inner readiness of the teacher for his/her task through qualities taken from his own experience as well as what he has been able to glean from his intensive study of Rudolf Steiner's educational and other works.

This book, now available for the English reader through the superior translation by Dorit Winter, conveys not only invaluable information but may also enkindle a real joy for the teaching profession – whether in a Waldorf School or in any other type of school!

Virginia Sease, Ph. D.
Goetheanum, Switzerland, February 2012

1. The School Building, or the Art of Attentiveness

Anyone who has ever entered an empty school building experiences a particular atmosphere. It's as if you sense the presence of the children and students even though they're not there. It's like observing a wrapping that has retained the imprint of its contents. You look around, walk through the halls; there's a hollow echo; here and there a coat hangs on a hook. Children's paintings have been hung along the walls. A tall sculpture stands in the entryway. When you get to the main hall, you feel as if it were filled with expectation. When you get to the faculty room, you sense what has taken place there: over here a stack of main lesson books, over there an open notebook, along the window ledge a few plants, some cared for, some pathetically neglected. The entire impression is of the imprint of daily life.

On a different occasion, you enter the school in the morning, just as the children are arriving. Everything brims with life. Children stream through the halls hurrying to their classrooms. Then all is quiet; the lessons have begun.

A teacher walks down the hall. He is entirely wrapped up in the lesson he is about to teach. All he sees is the doorway he's about to enter. He could also see the coats lying on the ground, but he knows they don't belong to his students, because his own classroom is further down the hall. He also sees the broken handle of the closet. Swiftly the thought passes through him, that he really should do something about this, and oh, yes, some of the hooks for the children's coats are also broken, with the result that jackets are piled upon jackets. Now that winter is coming, and the children will be wearing lined overcoats, these hooks really will have to be repaired. Otherwise too many coats will be lying on the floor or on the chairs. These thoughts dart through his head only because he happens to be seeing it all again. Now he has reached his own door. Does he really smell that toilet again? It's always the same with the boys from the other class. Finally his hand is on the door handle to his own room and he enters in eager anticipation, still half thinking of the building and grounds man who should be notified. But these thoughts fizzle out because 36 happy faces are now looking at him.

Two hours later the main lesson is over, and the children surge into the schoolyard, the teacher following along. He plays with the children, gulps some coffee, and looks around. He realizes that he can look at the schoolyard in two ways: he can observe the children and get a sense of the whole scene, or he can look it at all with the eyes of a stranger. What is he *really* looking at? Aren't the bushes completely trampled? Isn't there truly a lot of rubbish scattered throughout the yard?

He begins to pay attention to what he is actually

looking at. And a feeling of responsibility, of being co-responsible for the entirety of the school, connects—as if by itself—to his heightened attentiveness. Then it occurs to him that there are colleagues, (usually the older ones), who feel this responsibility, and who deal accordingly. They don't make a fuss as they pick up a piece of paper, or hang up a fallen coat, or make sure that some small repair is taken care of.

The teacher resolves to cultivate this somewhat more objective perspective. From now on he tries to look more carefully at the school building during the breaks, instead of going about his business habitually. Now he is attentive not only to what is happening in his own classroom, but to what is going on all around him. After a while, practicing to remember (though sometimes forgetting), he gradually acquires a new habit of attentiveness and—perhaps to his surprise—discovers that he enjoys this new capacity. The feeling of co-responsibility no longer oppresses him in the least; on the contrary, it gives him fresh energy as a teacher.

When you've lived in the same surroundings for years, it's perfectly natural not to look at everything carefully; after all, it's all so familiar. Only some extraordinary event excites interest. That can also happen in teaching, because day after day you see the same faces. But if you practice wakeful observation for apparently unimportant details, you strengthen your own presence in the teaching. It's as if you were sending forces of the "ego" [see glossary] into your senses. If this becomes a habit, you will also notice the changes in the faces of the children, indeed, the changes in the children overall. You will have achieved quite a lot from a seemingly trivial activity.

2. The Classroom, or the Mirror of Habits

Once you have acquired this new perspective, return to your own classroom after a day of teaching—or better yet, after a weekend—and you will be astonished. You will see your own habits spread out before you in the classroom. Everything is orderly: the desks are lined up; everything is in its place; the floor is not littered with paper; the paint brushes are all hanging where they should be hanging; the blackboard is spic and span; children's paintings adorn the walls in artfully composed rows.

Well, yes, but if I look at this scene with the gaze of stranger, I may have to ask myself: does any learning take place here? Or am I perhaps so neat and tidy that I am actually a … pedant? Or let's say I return to the classroom after a weekend nursing a secret anxiety that unimaginable chaos is awaiting me: desks, with notebooks piled on them, are scattered helter-skelter around the room; pencil shavings litter the floor; eurythmy shoes are flung about; cobwebs of dust swirl between the dried-out flowers which were placed on the window sill three weeks ago; the walls are lined with school work that is two months old; and the blackboard bears witness to the struggle for pedagogical survival. Before reaching for the broom with a deep sigh, it dawns on me that any true learning is impossible in this classroom, for I am, truth be told, a ... slob.

Ultimate self-knowledge can arise by opening a closet in the classroom and peering inside with these newly-developed eyes of a stranger: am I someone who masters the lesson through his habits, or am I someone who is constantly limping to catch up?

Now and again we take colleagues from another school on a tour through the classrooms of our own school and everyone sees and feels where the right balance exists between life and order. How to characterize this? Is there a lively orderliness, or a controlled disorderliness? In any case, we can hope to see the expression of children's activity, of liveliness expressed by the silent witnesses, the things themselves.

No matter what the case is, the teacher has the privilege of having before him a continually changing mirror in the form of his classroom. If he is able to see his workshop with the eyes of a stranger, he can glean a pearl of self-knowledge about his habit life.

This self-knowledge makes it possible for him to attempt to change something in some area where a change is required. But characteristic of our habits is that they are usually carried out unconsciously. Habits are etched deeply into the habit body. Once you've learned how to brush your teeth, you don't need to think about it anymore. We can ride our bikes and drive our cars only because we no longer need to think about how we do it; our actions are automatic. Anyone who wants to change the smallest aspect of himself in these realms will discover how difficult it is. But this is a realm of great importance for the teacher. If he decides to change some small detail of a habit, he will tap into the very forces that underlie all habits. Such forces are then released from their fixedness. They are enlivened and are once again mastered by the "I". It's a healthy process, of which we are not, at first, aware. But the result is that in our daily life, and thus also while we teach, we become more flexible, and no longer react in the same old way when some familiar situation arises. Then, when a child is naughty, the teacher may be able to react without the usual habitual reproach, but instead with an original response, perhaps even with a joke. In turn, such a response can have an enormously vivifying effect on the atmosphere of the class.

A teacher who can bring this element of flexibility into his own habits will be a blessing for his students.

But how do you recognize whether your habits have become "stiff"? In your own soul you can actually begin to notice something like a faint disgust for the routine of daily life in the classroom; then, all day long, your soul will be on "autopilot" (which is sometimes really necessary, as, for example, when you teach while fighting off the flu).

A symptom of this "autopilot syndrome" is an uncommon fatigue resulting from your teaching. After a full day at school, you can feel *healthily* tired: that's the sort of fatigue that regenerates itself completely during your night's sleep. But there is a different sort of tiredness that results in your being continually in a bad mood, or experiencing the sort of fatigue that can be repaired *a complete break*. That's when your life forces need special care.

It should be emphasized that this realm is not tapped *solely* by changing one's habits. Many things come together here. There's one other important aspect.

After all, the soul has many attributes. One such characteristic, which is of importance for one's entire life, is whether the soul succeeds in being thoroughly devoted to whatever it is engaged in. You could also call such devotion enthusiasm, or joy, or whatever you want to name it. If the soul is working out of this source, then, strangely enough, you won't get tired. The energy you summon up will spread to the habit-body and will fire it up. So if we find ourselves tired out by our daily work, part of which is guided by our habits, we can refresh ourselves through ideational, spiritual exertion. We'll come back to this.

3. Colleagues, or the Virtue of Recognition

In any school, the teacher is always part of the whole, part of the faculty. It's a reality that comes to expression in many ways.

Let's attend a lesson. The teacher is teaching, the students are learning something: it's the sort of school day in which the classroom is humming like a beehive. We are, let's say, in a 3rd grade lesson. Let's just ask ourselves what the children actually perceive about their teacher. First of all, they see him as he appears, outwardly. Even though they see him this way, they are barely aware of it, for they are awake elsewhere. They "see" what he is at the level of his soul, they feel his mood. Is he friendly and calm, completely absorbed in their activity, or does he appear tired and tense, not quite engaged? Or perhaps he is nervous and rushed. In short, they are far more aware, "see" far more than we think, of what he presents of himself. But there is something else they sense: namely, whether he is at one with the whole. An example can clarify this. A colleague of our teacher enters the room to teach a track class. The two are friends. As soon as the new teacher steps into the classroom, the children "sense" this, as though the same stream were now embodied in a different form.

The current of warmth has not been interrupted. The colleague's lesson takes off.

In a different case, another colleague enters our teacher's class, but this time our teacher harbors considerable unexpressed criticism toward this colleague, perhaps regarding his handling of the lesson. What happens now? The children feel—unconsciously of course—a kind of frosty current. It's as though something alien had entered the classroom, and consequently the lesson won't run smoothly, it drags.

Another example: It's recess, and we are standing in the schoolyard with the children. Various colleagues are present. How do they relate to one another? Do they talk to each other genially about this and that as they watch the children at play, or do they stand on three or four separate islands in the schoolyard, the way they stand at every recess? This too the children perceive as they play. A child is teased. Does she turn to a group of teachers who are talking together, or to one standing apart and alone? A big difference in the recess mood.

From these examples we can see that it is a *pedagogical* task, if not a necessity, that every single teacher cultivate his collegial relationships.

That requires actually being able to recognize the other. A lot comes together here. But if you can find the strength to honor something in the other which you don't have in yourself, the effect is mighty. If you attempt this, you'll first encounter your own shadow, which can appear in many gradations. But you also learn to see what you usually don't see, namely the striving of the other. You begin to notice the difference between essence and semblance.

If you engage in this effort energetically, you can succeed in learning to love a colleague in spite of his oddities or failures. It's well known that love, rather than blinding you, actually removes the scales from your eyes. Heretofore unnoticed positive attributes will come to light. You'll be able to see the colleague as he actually wants to be; you'll search for and find those aspects in him that are developing.

There are practical ways to do this. If a colleague has presented something fine at an assembly, then make it a habit always to tell him so. If a colleague has done something good for the school community, let him know that you appreciate it, even if what he did was simply part of his duties. If you are not by nature inclined to do that, and yet you persist in trying, you'll notice that this effort too will yield new strengths. Strangely, you will begin to observe the effect of this strength in yourself: you will gain a healthy self-confidence. (It goes without saying that in carrying out these practices, proper moderation must be sought.)

How then do we handle justified criticism? A colleague squawks at the children like a crow, the children are completely confused. How do we address him on this? A colleague simply cannot keep the most rudimentary order in the hallway outside his classroom; another comes to the assembly with a pedagogically or artistically questionable presentation. How then to talk to one another? Do we wait for the faculty meeting, during which just this presentation is "tactfully" ignored?

At first we notice that even if we do nothing, something happens anyway: the colleague experiences himself as if isolated, a feeling of loneliness softly creeps over him. There are colleagues who, for the sake of the matter at hand, talk to the teacher in question. If he is strong, the conversation may go well.

But it is better to talk to this colleague because you like him. This is an attitude, which, correctly understood, harbors no sentimentality, but rather a natural collegiality and dispassionate attitude based on respect. If you mean it honestly, you can walk up to him during recess, and start the conversation.

There is, however, a condition: you can do this only if you yourself are willing to be critical of your own work. All work is a work-in-progress, and mistakes are merely a part of it. We should thus cultivate a sort of sympathy for mistakes.

Often there is a big gap between the personality of an individual teacher and the circle of the faculty as a whole. In recent years, it has been helpful for colleagues to meet regularly in pairs, so that they can talk together about their work. Another possibility is for teachers of parallel classes, or neighboring teachers, to become speaking partners.

These arrangements needn't necessarily be called a faculty meeting. It's more a matter of a small, informal opportunity for conversation. Class teachers need such exchanges, because for the most part they are so isolated. This sense of isolation, as well as the fact that our teaching is so connected to the "how" of our being, means one cannot assume that teachers will critically question their own work. Self-critique, however, is necessary for professional self-knowledge. Collegiality, properly understood, is more than a little helpful in this regard.

It is the school community's duty to make sure that each colleague has a speaking partner. In the best case, a climate of collegiality itself gives rise to this. The less that institutionalized organization is involved in such matters, the stronger the consciousness of one teacher for the other will be.

It was said earlier that "A lot comes together here". What was meant?

In a social setting, for example also in a faculty, we are guided so naturally by our own feelings, our sympathies and antipathies, that we hardly notice this guidance or direction. But what comes to expression in this way? Through our feelings, part of our destiny expresses itself. With whom do we have a relationship, to whom are we attracted, to whom are we not attracted? Here we are embedded in a network of forces of which we are not aware. Nowadays, however, it's necessary to achieve some transparency in this realm. To that end Rudolf Steiner provides a basic exercise: Call to mind an encounter with someone. What feelings do you experience in doing so? Is it an obvious sympathy (even if it arises very delicately) or rather a feeling of remoteness, of something unknown?

In the first case we take the new acquaintance as he is, and merely register his appearance. In the latter case, sympathy arises only gradually, as we become acquainted through our work, and we thus honor the work of this individual much more than his being. In the first type of encounter, according to Steiner, we can assume that in most cases we are dealing with an encounter between people who have known each other in a previous incarnation. In the latter case there is the possibility of a new encounter amongst people who do not know one another from prior incarnations. All the impressions are new; you feel yourself to be a stranger in the presence of the other, but your common work provides a mood of possibilities, a mood of new beginnings.

Just think of the effect on our social life if we were to seek insight—however so gently and cautiously—into this aspect of our relationships with our colleagues. Why do I get along so well with this colleague, never criticizing his oddities? Why am I so poor at getting along with this other one, even though his achievements are so laudable? Observations of this kind don't lend themselves to being discussed in a faculty meeting; they are subtle observations, questions for one's own soul, to be quietly pondered.

Social life, getting along with each other, is a mighty task in a school, and much work still needs to be done in this realm. What has been presented here is only meant as a basic approach, a start. If you concern yourself energetically with recognition of the other, if you are willing to scrutinize your own actions, and if you make an effort to be awake to the ebb and flow of feelings that arise from your collegial dealings, you will have created a basis for inner autonomy.

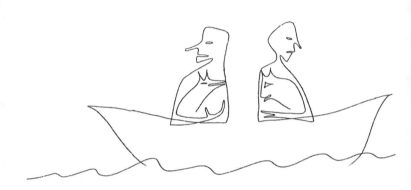

4. The Colleagues at the Faculty Meeting, or the Art of Listening

If, after a long faculty meeting, you've ever had doubts about the usefulness of such meetings, try to imagine that they didn't exist.

"Somewhere" in the office of a director, the fate of the school would be determined, and sooner or later you would find out how things are to be run in the school.

If you imagine this intensely, you'll realize: this is not how I want to work.

Why not? Because you'll realize, deep in your soul, that you want to share in the responsibility for the development of the school; for the school is a living organism, albeit guided by human beings. If you feel yourself to be responsible only for your own class, you'll notice, in the long run, that you are a foreign body in the school, no matter how good a teacher you are. The faculty meeting is the place where the development of the school as a complete entity can be discerned; it is the place where the faculty guides and motivates itself: it is the heart of the school. Nevertheless, the faculty meeting is not always the place for edification, for quickening, for energized activity. Why so? What is going on here?

Whenever we are in a large group of people, our individual conduct changes. If we were in a good mood before the meeting, no sooner have we entered the faculty room, or the room where the meeting is to take place, than a remarkable reflex arises in us: all day long we've been teaching; all day long we've been in charge; whatever happened was the result of our own preparation and our own determination to do as we do. Now, all of a sudden, we are no longer "I", but a part of the "we". "Let's see what they're up to today." It's as if you're not part of the proceedings, merely an independent observer. "Colleague X will dominate the meeting, so nothing will happen anyway." As if, in the meeting, collegial cooperation becomes opposition. "I never say anything anyway, that's the best way." It's true, a kind of courage is needed to speak up at the meeting; there's always the danger of being perceived to be stupid.

There's been a minor accident, because the handwork teacher always lets the children leave his class too soon. He really must stop this now! It is not right. It is not good. The matter is raised in the meeting. But what exactly gets said?

"By the way, let's remember not to dismiss our classes too early." It does really take a bit of courage to say things clearly in the meeting, even if there's the danger that you become the scapegoat.

"It's getting late and I have so much to do; in any case, I'll just take along a big stack of notebooks that need correcting." – The faculty meeting as multifunctional facility.

"If Colleague Z says such and such, I can guarantee that Colleague Y will say the exact opposite; and if Q says something, there's really no point in even listening anymore, because he always says the same thing, and he always drones on and on."

We not only find our habits mirrored in the classroom, i.e. in space. There are even more deeply-seated habits in our ways of thinking, in our habits of thought, in the habits of listening and responding. In conversations between one person and another, these habits are not perceived very consciously, because when we speak we usually pay attention to the content. But during our meetings, when we're also witness to a conversation, these habits come into sharp relief. The entire circus of human inadequacies can come to light in the most embarrassing and glaring way during faculty meetings. You can't fool the heart.

Such an experience can become so depressing that the faculty decides to look for new forms after it's been realized that more and more colleagues don't come to the meetings. The group is then divided into specialized meetings: lower school, upper school, special subjects, class teachers, administrators, and, in addition, the therapists. In short, fragmentation takes place to such an extent that the general pedagogical faculty meeting is hollowed out, completely losing its strength. Characteristic of this approach is fragmentation as a shadowy by product of individualization: In the end, everyone stands there alone. The big picture, the unifying experience of oneness, the identity of the school, gets lost.

A different reaction to the problem is the following: Mindful of the difficulties described above, and striving to make the meeting of interest to all, it can happen that the meeting is packed by overzealous attention to procedures, and a precisely planned flood of issues which can be handled only by those with the necessary expertise. Conversation ensues, but it is dead, and the meeting suffocates. It's no doubt a sign of the times that just this form of working together, which really is new, is so difficult to realize. What, in fact, was the original intention of this central point in the life of the school and its teachers? The intention was that the school would run itself through the accord of the active teachers. The faculty meeting, the vessel for this way of working, was intended to run the school, to enable the teachers to continue their own development, and to create unity, which only then could become the identity of the school.

On the evening before the start of the lecture cycle, *Study of Man,* began, Rudolf Steiner spoke about this matter:

"We shall not run our school in the way that a government department is run, but shall administer our affairs in a 'republican' manner. In a genuine teaching-community we cannot take shelter behind the protective cushioning afforded by a headmaster's rules and regulations, but must bring our own contributions toward the solution of problems in full personal responsibility. Each of us must be fully responsible for his or her deeds.

We will be able to create the possibility of replacing

a departmental administration by means of this prepara-
tory course, wherein we shall work towards grasping the
unifying elements of the school. Sharing this substance
in active participation will unite us in a common pur-
pose. (Rudolf Steiner: *Toward the Deepening of Wal-*
dorf Education, p. 76)

The spiritual image of the yet-to-be-born faculty meeting structure seems to be illumined by these
words. Steiner mentions administration, responsibility,
headmaster, and unity.

The Task of the Headmaster

The task of the headmaster is the spiritual work, which
the faculty accomplishes during the meeting and by
which the unity of the school community comes about.
The archetype is the shared work on the lecture cycle
Study of Man which at the time of the founding of the
first Waldorf School still took place under Steiner's spiritual leadership. Now we have the opposite situation:
the teachers have to summon out of themselves the spiritual strength needed to build community.

At that time, Steiner constituted the center which
radiated out toward the periphery of teachers. Nowadays the work shared by the periphery of teachers must
create the center: the school. So then, when a colleague
makes a presentation to the faculty meeting, perhaps
explaining how he has interpreted a pedagogical lecture, and, in addition a child study also takes place,
then the faculty is working in the realm of identity,

of unifying substance which, at the same time, entails continuing education for the faculty.

There will be a revivifying effect if, in this part of the meeting, new ways of working are attempted. For example, someone gives a brief introduction, which is followed by general conversation. Or perhaps three colleagues prepare the same material, and each of them speaks for five minutes on the theme, before a discussion ensues. Experience has shown that when we hear how the content was prepared in the souls of others, thus becoming "new", there can be a revivifying effect for all. Fundamental is the necessity of having each and every colleague make such a presentation, even if he refuses 100 times; because he has to do something for the first time once. We will get to the notion that for the efficacy of the faculty meeting, child study can have the same value as pedagogical study: because continuing education and the mutual effort and work create unity.

Responsibility for the Faculty Meeting

How do we maintain responsibility for the flow and content of the meeting? Whatever form the faculty has determined for the meeting, one thing is certain: all colleagues should strive to consider themselves as being equal.

We can bring this perception to mind by recognizing, at the start, that we are taking a step when we enter into the meeting. It's the same step we take during the day when we enter the classroom consciously: we leave our everyday self at the door. We try to be present, i.e. to be as we would like to be. We can also decide to be present for the sake of our colleagues instead of having our habits limit our attention; we can transcend those limits and listen for what is really happening.

Another way of helping can be as follows: there are always colleagues who speak a lot, those who speak little, and those who hardly ever say anything. Now, consider this situation, and try to gain some insight into what this actually means. You might be really interested, for example, to hear what a particular colleague has to say about something, but he offers nothing. Nevertheless, you notice that his silence does not signify disinterest. Should I call on him? Do I notice when I've talked too much, or when the conversation is on a dead-end track? In other words I try to "listen" to what is said, but also to what is not said.

Let's turn to the conversation. Let's try to listen to what's being said, not coldly, not abstractly, but rather in relationship to the person who is speaking. Let's try to listen to what he says, but also recognize how he says it.

Then we'll notice: I begin to be able to distinguish the merely personal part of what's being said, from what is truly meant. I am not deflected by the shell, but instead aim to discern the kernel.

This enables you to learn a new, active way of listening, which involves a kind of "thinking-with" the speaker. You can even have the feeling that you yourself are helping to structure the conversation, without ever saying anything. You become aware of two things: Remaining silent is not a sign of weakness; and you don't grow tired with you listen in this way.

Then, when you've practiced this for a while, a further question arises: when should I say something about the topic at hand? After all, teachers are prone to the bad habit of speaking before thinking in hope that the necessary thoughts will arrive as they speak. We can anticipate this through an inner question. For example: is now the right moment for me to speak up, or should I wait? Do I agree with what's been said, but merely want to hear it repeated in my own words? Or am I not at all in agreement, and should ask myself at what point to raise my objection? Do I want to make a remark which seems urgent to me, but which is actually not appropriate right now? In short, you step on the brakes, because it's always preferable to stop on your own than to be stopped.

This entire process described above, which takes place in the realm of self-education, requires inner courage: courage to continue, and courage to stay awake.

Here too, direct experience can show you that such self-control, practiced in shared conversation, doesn't weaken you; rather it strengthens you. Then, too, a consequence of this exercise is that when you do have something to say, you will choose your words more effectively.

There's another thought which can help me become a more receptive and constructive member of the faculty meeting. Before I raise my hand to speak, I ask myself the following: Do I intend to say something which really belongs to the conversation right now? Is what I want to say really to the point?

Of course each of us will say that we only ever speak to the point under discussion. It would, indeed, be somewhat absurd to declare that this wasn't the case. Nevertheless, in this realm we are often overcome by our own conversational tendencies; rarely are we our own masters. We could say that during the conversations of a faculty meeting a heightened activity of the sense of the ego of the other is required along with an intense fluctuation between "sleeping and waking", between perception of the other and perception of the self.

Only one thing can help us be more competent in this area, and that is to serve the matter at hand selflessly. In the meetings, a lot depends on whether we manage to watch ourselves while giving ourselves over completely to the matter at hand.

Finally, it should be noted that it's a healthy exercise to summarize contributions to the conversation as briefly as possible. Simply striving to do this is refreshing. A fundamental attitude for self-development, however, requires that none of the suggestions laid out above should ever be expected of others, but only of oneself. It's something else entirely, however, to raise the idea in the meeting of having the faculty attempt a certain inner attitude during the meetings.

Unifying and Developmental Aspects of the Faculty Meeting

At the end of the quotation cited above, Rudolf Steiner mentions the shared work which can unify the school. Such a remark can easily be misunderstood. What is the significance of having a group of people all striving for the same things? In earlier times, such a group, with common goals, might have given rise, for example, to the guilds, communities unified by common habits and customs.

Such life styles no longer serve us. In this regard, our own culture leans strongly toward the pole of individualization. But the common work alluded to above is a soul-spiritual activity. In this realm, unifying principles can work without impairing individual freedom. The school's identity can then arise from such common work. And what exactly is this identity?

The following experience may help clarify: We're sitting in the faculty meeting, discussing a problem that requires a decision. No one can figure out what to do. But the conversation continues. We attempt to clarify the basic aspects; we consider the consequences; and slowly, almost imperceptibly, the direction of a solution arises. The conversation continues, and suddenly everyone in the circle realizes: the solution has sprung up out of the conversation. The matter is decided, and it's agreed that in a week there'll be a follow-up to see whether the suggested solution holds water.

If you now review the conversational sequence, you find that no single contribution resulted in the solution; the review of the conversation reveals that the solution arose out of the conversation itself.

In this case, the community of assembled colleagues found the solution. In the community, more strength was at work than the sum of individual contributions could have provided.

This experience, though we don't have it every day, can bring about a feeling of good fortune, if the facts of the case are recognized. Is there something we can learn from this for our own individual attitude?

The meeting can be a place where the capacities of the colleagues resound together in such a way that they strengthen each other. The capacities of individuals work in the whole as in a chain, in which they "pass the 'golden bucket' from one to the other" (Rudolf Steiner). And there is another effect which you can observe in your own soul: you're proud of your colleagues, and you notice that you feel courage, that you are encouraged, to continue the common work.

What, then, comprises this identity, this "spirit" of the school? It is the common resonance of all the intentions, feelings, and thoughts of the people working in it.

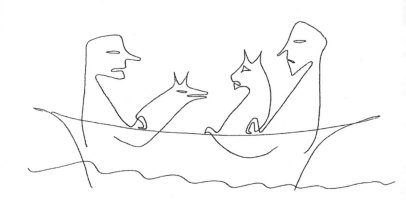

5. The School's Parents, or the Art of Being Interested

One of your colleagues has a class of 32 children. That's how many relationships he must now create with their families. It's one of life's facts that every single one of these families is fundamentally different from the next, also in their relationship to the school. And that's as it should be. We don't want to create a pedagogical monoculture consisting of parents who think just as we do. Nevertheless, it is good to unite the parents in a circle around the class; indeed, we are glad if the parents become interested in the school and its pedagogy. Perhaps we even hope the parents will collaborate with us. Many expectations surge this way and that, and questions concerning relationships with the parents occupy the teacher a great deal. It's an important realm that becomes ever more significant as the class grows older. But it's also a realm full of altercations and misunderstandings.

Let's look first at areas where parents and teachers can agree, before we look at areas of likely disagreement.

Like teachers, parents are educators. The former by culture, the latter by nature.

What does education mean for parents? It means

that they always want the best for their children. Whether parents ask this of themselves, or whether they also make this demand on the rest of the world, is up to them. Teachers also always want to offer the best, through their teaching, for the children entrusted to their care. And there's another point of agreement: in education you can never know what is best, because you can only partly anticipate how education will affect the future. In this realm there is no absolute certainty.

Whenever a human being is the object of a profession (as, for example, a patient is for a physician), you can never be completely certainty that the results of your work (in this case, the education itself) will actually bring about the best result.

Striving, or an intense hoping, is always related to the activity of educating. Educating is a path of self-education along which one is forever traveling.

That is why education and teaching are only partly a matter of technique (with their accompanying certainties). In education "doability" is possible only within a very narrow framework. Most of the time it's a matter of creative-moral activity. Or, in other words: when you teach you have to be inwardly present.

And, indeed, this also pertains to the parents; they too must hope that their educational attempts bring about the sought for results; they too are continually involved in self-education as they educate their children. But since the parents have, literally, a more natural relationship to their children, they are generally less conscious of this fact.

The teacher, however, is very much aware of this fact. He has to live with factors that he can't completely control; he has to live with a good bit of uncertainty. He can meet this only with honest striving and effort. Strangely enough, a remarkable paradox arises here: if the educator ever feels complete certainty in his pedagogical activity, he plummets out of the educational flow, the educational forces. Whoever engages in education from a perspective of certainty, actually no longer educates. Educating, as well as being educated, is a process, a journey.

In spite of that, parents and teachers want some basic certainty concerning the development of their children. Simply sharing this awareness can diminish the tension in the mutual relationship between teachers and parents. It means that parents can, without losing their trust in the teacher, acknowledge that he can make mistakes; it can also mean that the teacher completely accepts the biographical and pedagogical conditions of his students. If we grasp this in its full meaning, then the teacher's attitude will be: I want to face the child openly, I want an encounter with the child which takes the child's conditions and origins into account. This consideration is the basis for the maxim: at some level parents are always right.

At first such a statement will seem odd. But if you go into a parent meeting with this assumption, you'll notice that an openness results, and a real conversation can then take place. Of course this statement applies only in cases of a normal relationship between parents and teachers.

From the perspective of the teacher, this relationship should be professional: the teacher engages with the parents in a subtle balancing act in which he acknowledges the responsibilities he shares with them while remaining fully aware of the differences inherent in their tasks.

1. Parents in the School

One of the characteristics that make a school into a Waldorf school is the intensive collaboration with the parents. What is meant here is not just the working together on the school Board, or the parents' organization of the Christmas Fair, or even their baking of treats for school events; rather, what is meant is the sort of working together which unites the parents and teachers for the sake of the children's welfare.

A transparent working together can only arise if the parents are enthusiastic about what actually happens in the classroom; if parents have the experience: my child is happy in school. That's the basis: the experience that my child is happy.

But the question then arises: how do we bring this about?

After all, what happens behind the closed door of the classroom can only be described indirectly during parent evenings. Sure, some parents are able to read their children well enough to know how things are in school, whether they are thriving there, or whether some inexplicable pressure is weighing on them. Still, it's helpful for the overall relationship between home and school if the teacher enjoys sharing as much as possible about the lessons.

That can happen in a number of ways. In the lower grades, there can be parent mornings once or more a year, in which the children demonstrate for their parents something from their lessons. It doesn't always have to be recitation. They can show their parents something from the arithmetic lessons, or grammar or the foreign language classes, or, indeed, from any main lesson. You can end the morning with a shorter or longer class play.

You'll see that the children are delightedly ambitious in this endeavor. And if the teacher succeeds in tactfully enabling the weaker students to be part of the production, then such a morning can be of real benefit to the community of children and parents.

The children mightily enjoy this showing-what-we-can-do.

Basically, they too want everyone related to their class to know one another, to get along, to be part of a community. It's wonderful if at such parent mornings, you succeed in mixing individual presentations with presentations by the whole class. This type of parent morning can certainly be continued all the way through 6th grade.

In the middle grades of the elementary school it's best if this sort of activity is separated from the annual class play; otherwise it gets too unwieldy.

But you can do more. One day I realized to my horror that whenever a practicum student was visiting my class I taught differently. I behaved differently; I paid more attention to what I was doing, was, indeed, friendlier and more patient than when I was alone in the classroom.

I had to admit that I had caught myself in the professional liability of being only half conscious of my habits with the children. I had to recognize that my resolution, "to be only the person I wanted to be" when I entered the classroom, had become a mere thought. It was no longer a reality.

At the same time I realized that perhaps it was in this difference between the reality and the ideal of my teaching that seeds of distrust between teachers and parents originated. So as a sort of self-protection I decided I would no longer close the door of my classroom. Colleagues and teachers were always welcome to be part of the lesson whenever they wanted. The mutual awareness of the work proved fruitful. I was more the person I wanted to be and I overcame my secret fear of being observed. For the parents, however, it provided insight into the reality of teaching, and this experience not only gave them joy, but also showed them—far more than mere words would have—how things really unfold in the classroom.

I never observed that the intimacy, which life in the class also needs, ever suffered from this. What I did observe was that the students learned, in a very natural way, how to behave in the presence of visitors; the students were open, they were themselves, and they were friendly. They were as I wanted to be.

The behavior of the children developed in such a

way that whether there were visitors in the classroom or not, they always acted the same, just as *I* wished of myself. Let's call it the Pedagogy of the Open Door.

2. Home Visits, the Conversation

There is only one thing that can help me, as educator, overcome my prejudices vis-à-vis the parents, and that is interest in them. If I have 32 children in my class, then there are 32 (or more) parental homes offering me just as many portals and views of the world. And, as a teacher, I am greatly in need of such views. After all, the classroom ought not be filled with the stuffy air of narrow-mindedness, but aerated by the fresh breeze of the world.

With such an attitude, you'll go home after visiting a family feeling yourself very much refreshed. And it's to be hoped that the parents too have gained something from your visit, for you almost forgot to discuss the child, which was, after all, the reason for your visit. Suddenly we realize the truth of the sentence: *"... that as teachers we must be interested in everything in the world and everything to do with the human being. We must be interested in all worldly and all human things."* (Rudolf Steiner: Concluding words in *Practical Advice to Teachers*, GA 294, September 6, 1919) Parents are a big help in teaching us this.

Parents and teachers may be together for many years during the education of the children. This, too, is a reason for why it's essential that an enduring, fruitful relationship develop. We might ask ourselves the question, how necessary is this working together for the health of the Waldorf school? How necessary is a direct relationship between teachers and parents as part of the structure of a Waldorf school?

From the pedagogical point of view the situation is simple and clear: for any education it is best if the children have the conscious but clear sense that parents and teachers are pulling together on the same rope. This provides the child with the feeling of living in an integrated world, in a meaningful context. We protect the child from the experience of fragmentation, an experience that many adults need, namely of living in separate worlds simultaneously. For the being of the child it is important to grow up with an open mind. For that reason the child should also feel free to talk about school with an open mind, as we would about the experiences of life. If a little girl notices that her stories about her day at school create a particular effect, we already have a situation in which two worlds exist. For example: A child comes home from school and tells that it was a good day. Lisa was nice to her and Patrick was not as bad as she thought. But the teacher was a real dum-dum today and couldn't really explain the math. Well, that's just the way children talk about their day. It's as if they are taking off a soul-coat.

Now let's imagine two types of reaction. In the first type, the parents respond: "Gosh, really? Well, tomorrow will be better." The second type of parent says: "Is that really true? Does that happen often? His explanations are no good? What do you mean by dum-

dum? Is he unfriendly? Do you think he can't handle the class?"

These parental questions are all normal and warranted. The only thing is, the child just wanted to talk, and all these questions are somehow embarrassing, for she didn't really have an agenda with her report about the school day. This mood is, at least for the time being, unconscious in the child. But if through these sorts of question it becomes conscious, then the child experiences: home and school are two worlds, each with its own values and priorities.

To be sure, differences between home and school life constitute a fundamentally happy and fruitful reality. But there does need to be a bridge, and parents and teachers do somehow have to make an effort not to allow the pillars of the bridge to collapse, because if they do, the child will suffer. The child wants to love all the people in his world. That is the appropriate way of being for a child.

3. The Parents of the Class

In addition to this pedagogical perspective, there is also the social perspective, which should be briefly mentioned. It goes without saying that there are people who want an independent school. In the case of the Waldorf school, these are the parents. They are both overseer and client. The existence of the school is bound up with their will.

This fact is often noted, but rarely fully taken into consideration. We could, for example, do a lot more in conjunction with the parents in the realm of the class and its administration. It might be possible for parents to take an actively responsible role, for example, by having two parents represent the class, as is the case in many schools. Perhaps the teacher could meet with these parents on a regular basis to discuss the progress and development of the class. These parents, in conjunction with others, could in turn take on specific tasks. If some concerned mother and father had something on their mind, they could take it up with the class parents or with the teacher; they would have a choice.

For instance, the teacher talks to a mother, and he notices that she is stressed to the limit. He can then ask the parent representatives to get in touch with this mother somehow, so as to help her. An immigrant child is threatened with deportation; we have a lawyer among the parents, and we ask him for help.

Let's say something dramatic happens in the life of a family of a child in the class. The parent reps meet with the teacher to see how these people can be helped, perhaps by having the child stay with other families for a while.

Or: Parents in the class ask the parent reps for a conversation about domestic routines. (When does your child go to bed? How many hours a day do you allow your child to watch TV? How much pocket money do you give? How early must the child be home at night?) This is not a formal parent evening, but just a gathering at a parent's home. "Can you organize it so that the teacher also comes? He needn't give a lecture, but he might well talk about his own experience; he is, after all, also a parent."

A final example: The school year is almost over, perhaps we can have a relaxed get-together with the parents, possibly in someone's garden. No theme, just a chance to enjoy each other's company.

Of course there are also "difficult" conversations. There can be many different reasons for them, which we can't go into here. If such a conversation is imminent, the teacher can ask the concerned parents whether they would like someone else at the meeting, another father or mother from the class, perhaps, or a family member, or a friend.

The same thing can happen the other way around: as the teacher, I may want to have an "extra ear" present during a conversation, so I ask the parents whether there is someone who could join the meeting. (Of course, you are ready to supply a possible name.) At first, such a process might seem strange. "Who should be burdened with my sorrows (or my secret fears)? It's bad enough that the conversation even has to take place", you say to yourself. That's a completely normal response. But now try to realize that surrounding the class are parents whom you know, and whom you trust and about whom you realize: they will be there for "their" class's community. Wouldn't someone like that, who could listen to the discussion and help get things back on the right track if something sounded unfair, be a help? And if a conversation is not just difficult, but important, too, wouldn't that be sufficient reason to consider inviting a third party to the conversation? In short, by drawing upon a feeling of common responsibility between parents, parent representatives, and teacher, a social construct, a net of equal relationships can arise around the class. The professional authority of the teacher will never be undermined by such a social fabric. On the contrary, both parties will help each other grow. But this can work only if the core activity of the teacher—that is, his teaching—is transparent to the parents (other family members may also be interested) so that the parents feel: the way he is with us, that's how he is with the children. Transparency—especially in the teaching profession—requires accountability such that the parents feel: the teacher sees our child as he or she truly is. That is the basis for the relationship between the parents and the school. A lot can develop on this basis. Waldorf schools are an expression of civil society, i.e. the responsibility of the state becomes the responsibility of the parents. And that can happen only through collaboration. That is the background for Steiner's saying: *In this school, more than in any other, we need, if we are to move forward properly, more than a trusting working together with the parents. Our teachers certainly depend on finding this trusting working together with the children's parents because our school is built through and through on freedom.* (Parent evening of January 13, 1921, in GA 298)

It isn't always easy to describe this reality. How easily the misunderstanding could now result that, for example, parents in a Waldorf school must be obliged work with the school. That is not the case.

Everything originates on an individual basis. Some parents might say: I trust you with the education of my children, but don't bother us with anything else, because both of us have jobs. Inform us as necessary, but don't expect more from us. Other parents might get fired up about the Waldorf ideas, and want to become active in some realm. There are parents who approach the school very decisively, and want from the school exactly what they chose it for, but you will also meet parents who have found the school by chance, and who are satisfied with its style. Then there are those (rare) parents who actually know the kind of a school to which they're sending their children. All of these attitudes are justified, but they all have one thing in common: they expect something from the school and its teachers; they want the best for their child.

4. The Parent Evening

The first requirement for a parent evening is: it should be interesting!

Consider the fact that the parents often have just as much to do as the teacher, and yet we demand an entire evening of them. So the teacher has to offer something that's worth the effort.

It's important that the parents get an impression of how the school day really runs its course, but not just as an ideal. If, therefore, at a parent evening, the teacher reports on the life of his class, he should do so with as much liveliness and veracity as possible. And if, then, he gives examples that involve the children, and he mentions them by name, he should try to name them all. He might, for example, show a painting or drawing done by each child, and talk about each child's development.

Then he will be alluding to that aspect of the child which is developing, not the part that is problematic. I think it's tactless to indicate a negative aspect of a child when all the other parents are present.

Perhaps the teacher also wants to explain something concerning anthroposophical anthropology, such as the temperaments, or the four-fold human being, for example. Then it's important to take note of the following: Make sure you know what you yourself can vouch for in that anthropology. It's not sufficient merely to recite some superficial book-learning derived from anthroposophical texts. What the parents do find interesting, by contrast, is to hear what you yourself stand for.

You could ask yourself: which aspects of this anthropology have I already made a part of myself? Better to say that you don't yet understand this or that than to present something you have not yet worked through for yourself.

But how do we find certainty in our handling of anthroposophy? Let's consider this question.

Many colleagues, when first reading a text by Steiner, may have the following experience: it doesn't work to read Steiner's books and lectures in the way you read other books. The way you understand other books is through your cognitive comprehension of the content.

You have the content in your head, you know what it's about. When reading Steiner this is not enough. (We won't now consider the difference between the written books and the spoken lectures.) It's a common experience that if you "only" read, the content will not reveal itself to you; your thoughts will drift off. Then, too, you'll notice that spiritual scientific content, when read in the "normal" way, quickly slips from your memory. So we have to go about it differently. You'll notice: you have to *want* to understand the content. You have to stay with it, to concentrate. That can be accomplished if you read the same paragraph over and over, or if you try to create an image of the content, and then bring this image into movement again and again. In the lecture cycle *Study of Man,* pictures are, indeed, given — pictures that are supersensible in nature: Imaginations. In the lecture series entitled *Balance in Teaching* the pictures are not actually provided, nevertheless many are given throughout the text. For example: the image of the pre-birth forces that flow into the child through the head to form it sculpturally. These are then followed by complementary opposite forces that rise up into the head, there to collide with the incoming and descending sculptural forces. A wonderful, dynamic, supersensible image can arise in your mind. (See lectures 2 & 3 of *Balance in Teaching.*)

We might consider this pictorial approach as the first step in taking up the study of these elusive texts.

Now a second step: What happens if you have read the text in this way? You may, by comparison, be familiar with some music of which you are especially fond. You haven't heard or played it just once, you love to listen to or play it as often as possible. And each time it provides enrichment, refreshment. What is here true for art, namely that the soul wants to give itself over to an experience of it again and again, is also true for spiritual scientific content, because the soul yearns to take it up, but not through comprehension only. The second step, then, is repetition. You read the same text over again, then later you read it again, and "listen" for its effect on you. It's a rhythmical process. You could also call it meditation. You begin to live with the content.

The next step: you let the content rest. But inwardly it will continue to be effective. (In the Chapter Seven we will return to this question.)

Different issues come up at a parent evening. Who determines the evening's agenda? Certainly the teacher has a few things to say. But in the invitation that the teacher has sent out in a timely way, he can also ask for suggestions. These can then be passed on to the class reps, who, in consultation with the teacher, finalize the agenda.

During the parent evening we have to be able to engage in dialogue. If the teacher is responsible for a good part of the evening's presentations, and at the same time he asks the parents to participate, he may well be overextended, for he is now both moderator and presenter. Perhaps one of the parent reps can be asked to moderate the meeting. The teacher will then have greater liberty to make contributions, and the parents will feel involved as equals in the running of the evening.

Needless to say, such an arrangement requires that the evening be previewed with the class representatives. If we invite parents to participate in the life of the class in this way, a new relationship to the parents will come about, a relationship of mutual striving. The possibilities described above are merely suggestions for how the parents can become more involved in the communal life of the class.

If the teacher has question about his own teaching, there is great value in having him inform the parents that he would like to talk to them about it. His competence won't be questioned. For *"fundamentally, teaching and education are merely a special case of human interaction"*. (Rudolf Steiner in *The Renewal of Education*, GA 301, lecture 3, April 22, 1920, Basel)

If, then, with such a background, we ask the parents to help out on a class trip or a class play, they are less likely to grumble that they are allowed to help only when they are needed, that they are called upon "only" for their services as volunteers.

For many colleagues, especially the young ones but also the older ones, a parent evening means significant stress because they have to justify (though not explicitly) their work. And this work is deeply rooted in their entire being. Such stress can result in their filling the evening with their own voice. Just think, however, that many parents will then leave with unfulfilled expectations and return home muttering, in the best case: "Typical teacher!"

Another consequence of the above-mentioned tension can be that you present the lessons only in their ideal form, or (as is often the case in the high school) you talk only about the big picture of the lessons. Certainly we can, indeed, fire up our own enthusiasm in this way, but the relationship to what really happens in the class should never be ignored. It's the combination of both perspectives that makes it all interesting for the parents and for the teacher.

5. Summary and Outlook

There is only one factor determining the relationship of the parents to the school: the quality of the teaching. This is what determines everything to do with working together. Visualizing this working together shows us something remarkable.

Let's imagine the organism of the school as consisting of three parts. First we see the sphere of external conditions, the logistical realm. In the school certain things must be done if the life of the school is to run its course. For example, the buildings must be maintained, cleaned, and repaired. The administration must function smoothly.

Then comes the breathing aspect. In this breathing the life of the school takes place: the teaching, the life of the various classes, the activities of the kindergartens, of the lower, middle, and upper grades, of the pedagogical meetings – in short, the life of the school as a whole.

Finally, there's the realm in which the business of the school, with all its committees, councils, and advisory groups is conducted. Here, also, we have the management of the school, the board of trustees, the integration of all-school committees, and so on.

We can see that parents are involved with the school mostly in the first and the last realms. That's as it should be. Yet the area which can inspire and enthuse them—the middle sphere—is the least accessible to the parents. They experience this realm only indirectly, through their own children. We are actually expecting something impossible, in the long run, from parents who help on the board but don't themselves receive any "nourishment" from the school.

This is a weak spot in many Waldorf schools. Parents who are ready to work as volunteers should be nourished directly by whatever can enthuse them. If such an experience is not possible, or if small complaints about the life of the school start to sneak in—often through second-hand experience—the entire organism of the school is weakened. We need to find ways to engage parents with activities out of the middle sphere of the school's life, so that they feel enthusiastic for the education their children are receiving as described in the various examples above. We could also say it's a matter of the right interplay between the school and the parent body. If we strive for this, then we spare ourselves the socially problematic divisions: between parents who supposedly have "enough anthroposophical knowledge," and those who don't, or between parents who are "for" the school and parents who (without quite saying so) are not. We should move away from all of these irrelevant labelings.

Why is all this so important? In my estimation it is very important because: What, after all, constitutes quality? Quality is not something you have from the start. The question of quality is closely connected to the question of the developmental capacity of an organism.

I would like, here, to voice the thought that the development of the Waldorf school impulse—in other words the quality of the school—is closely connected to a change in perspective regarding the parents. Parents and teachers are equal partners, albeit in different realms, when it comes to the education of the children. Thus, it is valid for the faculty to include them in the pedagogical life of the school (which does not mean to include them in the pedagogy *per se*), and not simply relegate them to areas of service on the periphery of the school organism.

Rudolf Steiner's remark that the *"soul content of humanity is in the hands of those cultivating youth, the educators"* needs to be understood as being a shared responsibility between parents and teachers. (*The Renewal of Education*, GA 301, lecture 4, April 23, 1920)

6. THE STUDENTS, OR THE ART OF BEING INTERESTED IN EVERYTHING THAT IS GOING ON IN THE WORLD

Let's return to the classroom. We teach, are busy with the children, talk to them, work with them as a group and individually, tell a story; in short, we're in the middle of the life of the class. Now let's think of our class as a focal point uniting all the connections which the children bring together.

The child's family members are indirectly present in the classroom, as are their friends, neighbors, the neighborhood where they live, yes, perhaps even the town or the region. All these relationships flow into the classroom we share. In this little classroom we are thus connected with a fairly large part of the surrounding social reality. But: how aware are we of the social reality that stands in the background of each child? Do we feel ourselves connected to it as well? Karl's mother is ill: how will I relate to Karl? Lisa's older brother has left for Europe: what will I say to her? Peter's father is unemployed: how do I relate to him? Barbara is moving, but thank goodness she is staying in the school: how will I support her? Unfortunately a student has had to leave the school: how will we say farewell? In this way the life of the class surges through me; I am connected to it all.

In some way I am co-responsible for this surging life, with its waves crashing against the door of my classroom. Not necessarily in the sense of being actively involved, but rather in trying to have a mirror inside myself, which can reflect the multifaceted aspects of life surrounding the class. I look into the mirror. Whatever I see, that's what I carry in myself. Not by suffering on account of it, but because in this profession I have the opportunity of being connected to many people.

An opinion that easily gains currency in the life of the school is that it's best not to ask the teacher, because, after all, he already has too much on his shoulders. Better to shield the teachers, because they are, fundamentally, overburdened. This can intensify to the (unexpressed but highly effective) assumption and opinion: a good Waldorf teacher is overworked.

If you don't have a fully loaded schedule of meetings, you can't be fully engaged, you aren't really committed.

Needless to say, everyone is free to organize his life as he wishes. But what's important here is to realize that such "pictures" and ideas are damaging for the school. A school flourishes when in relates to its surroundings through an active breathing process. That implies that we can have other "pictures" of the faculty, such as the following: The teachers in this school are committed to their work, but if, once in a while, we want something from them, they are here for us, too.

Every now and then they may even enjoy doing something unrelated to school.

Another peculiarity can be noted here. When Steiner discusses the conditions for becoming a student of spiritual science—namely, to feel oneself to be a part of the whole—he gives an example which is of particular importance for the pedagogue. He describes a situation in which a teacher is dissatisfied with a student's accomplishment or behavior. Instead of looking for the cause in the pupil, as would be customary, the teacher is to practice looking for the lack of accomplishment, in himself. We are dealing here not only with an important principle of all pedagogical activity, but this example can also help us to understand what is meant by the sentence: feel yourself to be a part of the whole, especially in relationship to pedagogy. How are we to understand this more specifically?

When as a teacher I teach the children something, a child takes up not only the content of what I am teaching but also the "how" of it. And this "how", as we well know, makes all the difference. But where does it come from? It originates in the soul of the teacher, in his handling of the material, in his originality. This expresses how he relates to the world (the material) and the child (the "how"). The teacher mediates aspects of the world that have passed through his own soul, to the child. He is a mediator. If then, I, as teacher, feel myself strongly connected to the world, if I am interested in what is happening in the world, if I experience myself to be part of this world, then the "how" will have a different coloring than if I limit myself only to the classroom. If what I teach doesn't really "take" the way I had hoped it would, I ought to ask myself what's going on with myself, instead of complaining that the students haven't understood what I wanted them to learn.

This fact is also inherent in the well-known experience that any subject matter requiring of the teacher, for whatever reason, extra effort will be taken up by the children more strongly than content which no longer challenges the teacher. This also resounds in the "Principle for the Teacher": namely, that they should be interested in the big as well as the small world. That is also one of the reasons for having a certain complexity in a class community; there will be simply more life in it.

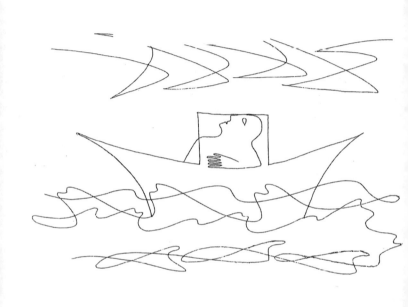

7. PREPARING THE LESSON: THOUGHTS, FEELINGS, ACTIONS

In the records of the faculty meetings with Steiner at the Stuttgart school, there is the charming moment when he asks the teachers, with great restraint, whether there is any truth to the rumor going around that the Waldorf teachers sleep only from 5:30 to 7:30am since they need the rest of the night to "prepare". And, he goes on, if that is the case, might they not find going to sleep already at 4:30am to be a useful remedy? We can hear a gentle, exceedingly friendly irony in the question. We can also hear, from his follow-up questions, his astonishment that preparations are really experienced as being so difficult. He then asks the various teachers to report on how they do their preparations. (*Faculty Meetings with Rudolf Steiner*, GA 300b, Meeting of January 23, 1923)

Sure enough, the oddest ideas cluster around the question of the proper way to prepare one's lessons. That's quite understandable when you consider that the teacher's preparations, more than most practices, are completely dependent on his personal attitude, temperament, and character. On that account, it is not easy to generalize about this theme. Still, let's give it a try.

Whenever we want to prepare a particular lesson, there are two realities to take into account: the children and the material. At first these two seem to have nothing to do with each other, they are alien to each other. This polarity creates a tension. It's an artistic tension comparable to the tension you feel before stepping out on stage, a sort of stage fright. For some this feeling of tension can be a real torment, whereas others come to realize that they need it. We have to reconcile these polarities. How can we go about doing so? First, we try to consider the material: what does it contain, where is my point of entry, where is a riddle? Here, too, I will find that no matter how simple or complicated the material is, I must try first of all to consider it in such a way that I become enthusiastic about it. That will engender joy, as I consider the material and try to organize it, try to make it transparent. Joyful anticipation will come about as I think about teaching this to the children. Have I achieved this enthusiasm, do I then also become inwardly active?

A lot depends on the answer to these questions. Your own experience will confirm that the way you teach—the freshness, the newness, the as yet undigested portions of the material—affects their health. Steiner tries to show the teachers how to prepare their lessons, not only in his lectures, but also in the faculty meetings. Two weeks after the scene described above, he returns to the theme of preparation. What he says there again is intended to motivate not merely the mind, but the whole human being. We can read these puzzling words over and over, and again and again the experience will spring from them: *"However, in order to have healthy school children, the teacher must understand the art of mastering himself. You should really try not to take yourself, that is, your own private self, into the classroom, but you should have a picture of* **what you yourself become by virtue of the subject matter** *you are going to deal with in whatever lesson you teach. Then the subject matter will make something of you.* **What you yourself become through your subject matter has an extraordinarily enlivening effect on the whole class.** *The teacher ought to feel that if he himself is indisposed, his teaching overcomes the indisposition, at least to a certain degree, then he will have the best possible effect on the children. He should teach out of the disposition that* **teaching is good for him;** *that whilst he is teaching he changes from being morose to being cheerful."* [*emphasis added*] How realistically Steiner viewed this can be gleaned from a comment he made right after the passage just quoted: he hoped that the children, upon arriving at home, would not have to swallow some substance to make them throw up because they were unable to digest the lessons they had enjoyed that day in school. [translation in part by Steiner Schools Fellowship Publications] (*Faculty Meetings with Rudolf Steiner*, GA 300 b, Meeting of February 6, 1923)

Anyone who teaches knows the truth of the saying: we may be too tired to teach when we start, but by the end of the day we'll notice that we feel perfectly refreshed.

And what is the children's role in this? I see them in my mind's eye: what will happen if I do this or that?

73

Should I do something to surprise them? Or should I start with something familiar, and then introduce a completely different direction? There are no rules here; it's a process you go through.

An experience may elucidate the relationship between the subject matter and the children: After a (short) holiday, the first day of school was looming. I wanted to begin with a math main lesson, and nothing at all was occurring to me. The subject, all this calculating, disgusted me.

So I went to sleep unprepared and with a bad conscience. Somehow I got through the next day of teaching.

That evening, when after a full day with my students I sat down at my desk again, my inner mood was entirely changed. Ideas bubbled up like anything and new "arithmetic-wonders" were noted in short order: enough preparation for an entire week. It really was as if I had grown into something through the subject itself. The whole human being is active if he engages with the material and the children in his preparations; thoughts and feelings become the force behind the deeds and actions which arise the next morning. It's a truly healthy process, and its quality is not necessarily dependent on the length of time devoted to it.

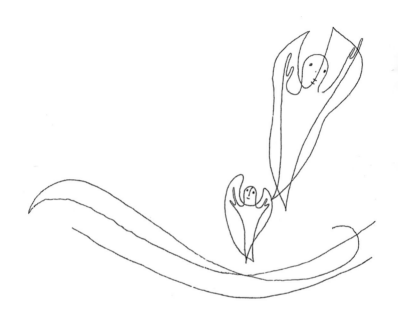

8. Concerning Primary Sources, or the Virtue of Veneration

The question is often raised: Is the concept of the Waldorf school as a whole contemporary? For many people Rudolf Steiner is, after all, a historical personage, not an inwardly living one, and hence he is perceived to be no longer appropriate for the 21st century. Are the schools, nonetheless, modern?

These questions are certainly justified, and everyone should find his own answer. Some thoughts on this topic might be helpful.

To arrive at an answer to this question, it's good to remember that in the realm of the Waldorf schools, we have to distinguish between the impulse underlying this school movement and the different forms it has assumed. The impulse is a force that anyone can sense who is open to a child-appropriate education and the thought that the human being originates in the spiritual world. In other words, this impulse is relevant as long as there are children.

The forms that a Waldorf school assumes are related to the culture, the habits of the place and time in which it originates. This was how the first Waldorf school in Stuttgart was seen, namely as a particular form chosen at that time. In short: These forms are time-dependent and can change according to the cultural circumstances.

This is an important point. If you don't distinguish these two realms, you are in danger of confusing form with impulse. If that happens then paralysis and dogmatic attitudes arise, and the accusation of being a cult rears its head. In this regard there are already several practices in Waldorf schools that give me pause for concern. For example, it is said that the seasonal table in the corner of the classroom should exemplify how the classroom is supposed to look to make it Waldorf. But that is not the case. Others will say: the school day is supposed to start with a so-called rhythmical part ("morning circle"). That is a questionable form if the consequence is that the latter portion of the lesson, the so-called working part, is no longer rhythmical. All forms which somehow begin to have a life of their own, and are even seen as determining the identity of a Waldorf lesson, must be questioned: where do they originate and are they really still an expression of the deeper impulse?

Similarly, the idea has taken root that a class play is mandatory at the end of 8th grade. And yet no one can tell you why that should be the case. Why not a class play in the 5th or 6th or 7th grades? Why not in the 2nd or 3rd or 4th grades? Why this alignment of views concerning the 8th grade? You can often see that so much energy is spent on this, that a truly mighty production of high school proportions results, reaching far beyond the soul capacity of the children. In addition, this is how social deformities come about in the school: every subsequent 8th grade must now come up with a bigger and even mightier production. More frequent productions, but with less extravagance, are healthier. It is better for the children, because it is more appropriate for children, and doesn't overextend them. Here, too, the question arises: where does such a "form" originate? And why isn't it discussed?

Let's ask the question again, but this time in relation to the subject matter. Here Rudolf Steiner provides a relevant stimulus for our thinking when he says that we should distinguish between two types of subject matter. One kind of subject is necessary for the child's development, the other comes from the expectation of the culture we live in. The latter may be deleterious for the child, which is why the art of teaching requires that the teacher transform it into something healthy. (*Practical Advice for Teachers*, GA 294, lecture 1)

How are we to understand this statement, if we are to grasp it in a lively way? Surely it means that the subjects can change without compromising the impulse. That, however, would mean that a Waldorf school is thoroughly capable of change without loss of identity.

This tension between what is wanted and what is required has been a fact of life in the Waldorf schools since the founding of the first one in 1919. Let's look at how reading and writing are taught. It's a cultural necessity, the children must learn this. Steiner determined that the conventional method of learning these skills was inappropriate for a 1st grader. Therefore he developed a didactic detour which bends this subject into a healthy activity (while retaining the right to spend more dedicated time on it than usual). What sort of situation do we find ourselves in today? Society demands that the children learn to manage computers. But we experience this as being unhealthy for the children. So we find ourselves in the same situation as with learning to read. The task is clear: we have to find a way to take up computers in such a way that no damage is done to the children. How do we find our way to such a method of teaching? I venture to say: through appropriate, living imagination; in the language of the *Philosophy of Freedom*: through "moral imagination".

These examples show us that the study of primary sources, Steiner's statements, does not fixate but encourages development and will lead us forward.

This kind of striving will then lead, seemingly of its own accord, to the conclusion that the sources—properly seen—attain more and more relevance. Personally, I've experienced how most all of the present-day problems that schools face are already addressed in the pedagogical lectures and the transcriptions of the faculty meetings. The latter are a treasure trove. For the teacher, they are the equivalent of the book that Rudolf Steiner and Ita Wegman co-authored for the physicians: both texts present the archetype of pedagogical development in society.

For a further example, let's take another look at the text of the faculty meeting of February 6, 1923 (in GA 300b). After the text cited above, on how to deal with the various subjects, Steiner says the following: *"And if I were to say something about this in a positive vein,*

I should still have to keep on stressing that it would be highly desirable—though I know that ideals cannot be fulfilled immediately—that Waldorf teachers teach without any notes, that they are really so well prepared that they don't need to have recourse in any way, during the lesson to something they have written down. For that vital inner contact with the pupils is immediately broken if the teacher needs to look at his notes. He should really never have to do that. That is an ideal." [translation from Steiner Schools Fellowship Publication, 1988]

We read a sentence like that. What does it stir up in us? "Sure, the older teachers, they can do that, but not us, it's an ideal. It really does not disturb my teaching if I have my own preparations in front of me. Let the students see that I, too, need something to be able to teach", and so on. But how is it really? I'll describe a hypothetical but not entirely unrealistic lesson, perhaps a foreign language class. At the beginning of the lesson, several verses are spoken, a poem is recited or perhaps a song is also sung. Then the "learning" begins. The lesson is given with the help of copies out of a soiled booklet; there are questions on the paper to be answered. These questions couldn't be more stupid ("This evening I'm going to the movies. Do you want to come?" and such like); in short, the lesson tires the teacher, while the children, looking as if paralyzed, yearn to find an escape from the lesson. ("Today the children can't concentrate!") The class crawls toward the redeeming bell.

Now I observe a 10th grade math class in a different

school. The teacher enters the room (without a brief-case!), writes an equation on the blackboard, and asks for suggestions on how to solve it. A lively conversation unfolds about what could be done. He follows the students' suggestions, shows the correct and incorrect solutions, follows their suggestions with new equations on the blackboard as a result of their answers; he works out the solutions while the students try to solve them in their notebooks. Wrong directions bring on heartfelt laughter, and he shakes ever more tasks out of his sleeves, and puts them on the board. At the end he summarizes the whole lesson with a short dictation, assigns some homework, bids them farewell in a friendly fashion, and disappears. No trace of fatigue in the classroom, instead, a deep in breath, full of admiration (already apparent during the lesson).

There, I saw it with my own eyes: Steiner is right!

Here was a lesson that flowed directly from the teacher into the students, and did so in thinking, feeling, and willing. Through this lesson I also saw how the teacher grew into something through the subject he had "embodied". And if, then my bourgeois stooge says, "I'll never be able to do that!" then I remember the illuminating words, *"There slumber in **every** human being faculties by means of which he can acquire for himself a knowledge of higher worlds."* (First sentence from *How to Know Higher Worlds*, GA 10, emphasis added) [translation from Anthroposophic Press, 1947]

If we try to see Steiner's primary texts not as a collection of static facts, but as an invitation to self-development and experiment, then we can experience them as a mighty source of power. Then the stultifying specter of historical Waldorf precedence falls away and we are left with the overwhelming impression of living spirit. This can arouse in the soul genuine admiration for the deed of the founding of this impulse, which took the form of the Waldorf school. May every teacher commit himself to this deed.

9. The Lesson, or Gratitude for Life

I would now like to represent the point of view that "school"—being allowed to be with children on a daily basis—can be taken up as an enviably good and healthy profession.

This may sound like a joke, given that teaching is often portrayed as the opposite: namely, as a difficult, stressful, thankless profession. Indeed, many countries suffer from a lack of teachers, or at least the threat of a shortage. Nevertheless, the point of view I wish to represent is that by renewing the teaching profession through spiritual science, it is precisely this profession that can be given a fresh boost. If only we could see the art of teaching as a challenge to ourselves instead of a set of prescriptions, honor would be restored to this profession.

First, though, we must bring to mind the deterrents to this profession which have arisen in our time, also within the community of Waldorf schools. Whether this applies more locally, or in general, shall be left up to the gentle reader.

Let's note the following "problem areas" and provide a brief commentary. Then I'd like to try portraying them in a different light:

1. The idea of the art of education is bound to be misunderstood in our time, and stands opposed to the idea of what is doable.
2. What, in our day, is meant by the vague notion of "pedagogical relevance"?
3. There is also a lack of unanimity about the meaning of the words "intellectual achievement".
4. The reality of the class as a community and the related questions of class size and needs for individual attention (differentiation) present us with an urgent problem.
5. Incorrect ideas about the autonomy of the teacher are in circulation.

1. The Idea of What's Artistic and What's Doable in Education

Herbert Hahn, a first-generation teacher at the Stuttgart school, is once supposed to have asked Rudolf Steiner what he would do if he were to start the Waldorf school over again. Steiner is reported to have responded: "Everything more artistic." This statement lets us see the importance of artistic teaching, but what exactly is to be understood by it? Does it mean that drawing, painting, sculpting should fill every lesson; that we should produce a gorgeous main lesson book for every main lesson, and also for the track classes? That does not characterize the "artistic" in the lesson. Certainly, Waldorf lessons ought to have an esthetic component, since beauty does enable the soul to learn more easily and with more durability. But "artistic", in Steiner's sense of the term, is not thereby addressed. A mix-up is likely here, namely the confusion of "esthetic" with "artistic". If these two words are treated as being synonymous, then the so-called "Beautiful" becomes an end in itself, and no later than 6th grade it will disgust the children (all the way to the complaints of the high school students: "Oh no, not *another* main lesson book!"). If we want to gain an idea of "artistic teaching", we need to look for guidance in the pedagogy. When do we, as teachers, know that the lesson was successful? When it was so *alive* that the hearts and the minds of the students were touched. When the lesson ended with a deep sigh — as after any genuine experience. Everyone who has ever taught recognizes such a moment and will remember it with gratitude.

Often the factors of a successful lesson are ascribed to something like: "Today the children could really concentrate", or: "Things rolled along as if on their own." Even the day of the week or the weather conditions are believed to play a role in a successful lesson. However, these perceptions lack sufficient discrimination. Better to ask oneself: what were the factors contributing to success? If I can recognize them, I may have further opportunity to implement them.

One of the secrets lies in the answer to the question: what, then, constitutes a *living* lesson? It is a lesson that has been formed entirely out of yourself, so that the whole arc of the lesson is like a thoroughly penetrated composition. It's an artistic arrangement, in which the various ingredients which constitute the lesson (the subject, the goal of the lesson, the children, the day and whatever preceded this lesson, my relationship to the "how" of the subject), are all blended into a unique mixture.

Indeed, this process can be related to cooking. After all, cooking is also an art in which the goal is to create something, by various means, which is digestible and tasty. The strange thing is that before they are cooked, the various ingredients may be neither digestible nor tasty; as a matter of fact, in their raw state they may even be harmful. What is here true for physical nourishment can also be true for the process of learning, except for the fact that no substances are eaten; instead, something is taken up by the senses, and it has to be so well prepared that the soul can digest it. Learning is soul-nourishment.

One really should consider the meaning of the words "teaching matter", which, like the word "education" itself remind us distantly of nourishment, of growth: to educate – to raise. (This relationship is even clearer in Dutch. The literal meaning of education is: "raise nutritionally" – "*opvoeden*".) It would be superfluous now to think about the relationship between cooking and the musical process of composition. In any case, all the processes we've been considering include something artistic, which in the act of completion is unique. A teacher who copies and repeats a successful lesson knows from experience, that "something" which was present won't let itself be repeated; if one tries, what remains is a stale taste. It's like the second steeping of what was initially aromatic freshly ground coffee; it has lost both freshness and aroma. We should refrain from offering a second brewing to the children we are teaching.

This, then, characterizes the artistic element in our teaching. The importance of such artistry cannot be sufficiently valued. As with any nourishment, it will determine whether the lesson has a healthy or unhealthy effect on the community of students. In this regard the teacher, and the school, must not lose their grip.

In the final and fourteenth lecture of *Study of Man*, Rudolf Steiner considers the artistic effectiveness of the teacher in the light of a "categorical imperative": "Keep your imagination active." Anyone who does not want to do this, who permits himself to "grown sour", to become a "pedant", whose pedagogical accomplishments become "frozen up" through repetition, might be good for many things, but not for teaching. He should find a different profession.

This process-oriented, living teaching is subject in our time to the pressures of what is thought to be do-able in education. Even though the words are no longer used, the idea does (still) live that in the end learning is a matter of some sort of "input-output" mechanism. Unfortunately, the above-mentioned idea—that artistic teaching is well and good, but "real learning also needs to happen"—is also widely held. The consequence: spurred by fear that the children can't learn enough, we reach in Waldorf schools for ordinary methods, "just to be safe". Dealing with this demand has been complicated by the truly excellent methods that have now appeared in the market – original, comprehensive, and witty. But even the best methods have the same pedagogical consequence as the worst: they rob the teacher of the process of pedagogical creativity. Instead of bringing to the class an air of immediate freshness arising from what he himself has come up with, the teacher becomes the agent of someone else's (anonymous) content and forms.

If we want to strive for a society worthy of human beings—a society we prepare through the education of our youth—then we must allow this thought to flow into our education: namely, that the child needs the whole human being as model, so that learning remains a human enterprise. It seems to me that this sentence is especially significant for the future, in which the question will arise whether teaching should be taken over in part, or entirely, by computers. Or whether the class teacher should be replaced early on by specialists in particular subjects. A time will come when what is decisive for education in general will be whether there will still be teachers at all, teachers who will "give birth to" imagination through what they are teaching their students, and thus ignite in their souls the fire for love of the world.

It is of utmost importance that Rudolf Steiner emphasized the necessity of imaginative teaching not just for the little ones, but for students aged 11, 12, 13, and 14 years old: their awakening reason needs to connect to their entire soul life.

"Therefore in these years we should foster an intercourse alive with imagination between teacher and child. The teacher must keep alive all his subjects, steep them

in imagination. The only way to do this is to permeate all that he has to teach with a willing rich in feeling. Such teaching has a wonderful influence on children in their later years." (*Study of Man*, GA 293, lecture 14) [translation from online site: rsarchive.org]

What follows is an example to elucidate the "willing rich in feeling" in relation to the subject. A colleague has an 8th grade. He is about to begin the main lesson on the industrial revolution. Normally he would go back into the 18th century, to England: First spinning machine, first steam engine, first bridge made from cast iron, and such like. But he finds no joy in this traditional approach. Undecided, he walks through the town. Suddenly he notices an old street lamp made of cast iron. He sees something nerve-like in the iron, like a tree, he sees a flower-motif expressed in the iron, which can only have been made by weather boarding, and suddenly his curiosity is awakened.

He goes to the library and seeks out everything about the history of street lamps. After some research, a gripping panorama is spread before him, consisting of models and production of such lanterns, from the newest lighting fixture using electric lights, right back to the gas lantern. Now he has found an approach to the means of transportation in the 20th, 19th, and 18th centuries. To his surprise, he discovers that around the year 1850 there were hardly any paved roads; that the track widths in different countries differed, which often caused broken axels when the coach had to negotiate a different track. In short: he is in the midst of his theme, and now has the urgent wish to share with his students all that he has discovered. We can easily picture how eager his 8th graders are to take up these "discoveries". Learning and teaching have sprouted wings. Such experiences have a long reach; they work in remarkable ways. We can also say: every lesson creates the future.

2. Pedagogical Relevance

As mentioned earlier, the idea that there are two types of subject appears as the opening theme in Steiner's *Practical Advice* lectures: there is the subject matter which is necessary for the development of the children, and there is that which is either meaningful for social life, or required by it, even if it is meaningless, or even harmful for the learning process. The task then, is to form the lesson in such a way that whatever would otherwise be unhealthy is handled in such a way that it has a healthy effect on the children. Initially, this fact is represented in the polarity between learning to read and write, on the one hand, and arithmetic on the other. Because reading is a cultural "convention" which actually has nothing to do with the human being, the learning of reading requires a detour, so as to bring it into harmony with the human being, the child. Not so with arithmetic, which is an inherent human activity. In the latter case, such a detour is not necessary. (*Practical Advice to Teachers*, GA 294, 1st lecture, Stuttgart, August 8, 1919)

There is also the conventional wisdom concerning the differing subjects. It is important to try to get to the bottom of these conventions. It's not the art of education, but rather the conventions that need to be rethought from time to time: Are they still relevant to social life, to the children, and to young adults?

The faculty can also ask itself whether the time devoted to the various subjects in the schedule is still justified. After all, the schedule should be treated as an expression of the ever-changing life of the school, instead of as some kind of the dominating constraint that hangs on year after year. A few examples will make this clear.

As is probably known, stenography used to be part of the original curriculum, and in those days it was considered to be very progressive and modern. That subject has disappeared, for technological developments have made it superfluous. First aid for accidents, by comparison, is still relevant. An even more interesting example is the following: on February 5, 1924, during a faculty meeting with Rudolf Steiner, a handwork teacher regrets that painting in the upper grades cannot be carried out as regularly and continuously as in the lower grades. Steiner's answer is then as realistic as it is tactful in light of the young person's being: "It doesn't matter if painting is interrupted for a couple of years [!] and replaced with modeling. The basis is that painting continues to work in the unconscious, so that returning to it after an interruption can be carried out with vitality and skill. In everything to do with skill, it's always the case that if something is held back, there will soon be great progress, just because it has been interrupted." (GA 300c, faculty meeting of February 5, 1924)

Here we encounter an insight into human development which not only can be documented, but also recognized out of our own experience. (If you've ever tried to return to playing the piano after a summer vacation, you'll have been amazed by the agility of your fingers after such a long gap.) Here lies dormant the possibility to revitalize the upper grades curriculum, by introducing a rhythmical alternation of arts and crafts. But we can also review the skill building subjects in the middle grades, to see whether perhaps a different treatment, one that is less linear and less goal-oriented, might not have a healthier and more enlivening effect on the students. Let's look at a few examples. They are meant as food for thought rather than a definitive assertions concerning the subject.

It's a fact that nowadays elementary computer skills belong to these subjects. The actual question, however, must deal with the pedagogical relevance: when and how can these lessons be introduced so that more than mere skills (which most of the children have already acquired, anyway) are introduced.

If we observe the children, we might well ask ourselves, for example, whether recorder lesson after 4th grade have pedagogical relevance; does the achieved skill level enliven the experience? The musical children have already been playing an instrument for some time; orchestral groups generally have their beginnings in the 5th grade. Children who don't play an instrument need a different musical challenge. Another example: What would happen for the children if handwork were omitted from the curriculum at one point for a year? Or woodworking? Or gardening? Wouldn't there be an intense and joyful involvement with the subject if it were not a constant part of the weekly schedule? A true balance is achieved when the (joyful) experience of learning is felt to be related to achieved skills.

We should always be asking ourselves whether our lessons relate objectively to the lives of the students, or whether perhaps there is a certain compulsion that undermines its pedagogical effectiveness. And can it be that this compulsion arises because we follow the schedule, instead of forming it? Before we consider the relevance of a subject, let's characterize the concept: *"... that nothing should enter the lesson that is not, in one form or another, **to be retained for all of life,** instead of what is generally done today, including only whatever coalesces into skills.*

(...) This is what will characterize the education of the future most strongly, that all these things which are brought to the child, will also remain with that human being for all of life." (*A Social Basis for Primary and Secondary Education*, GA 192, lecture 1, May 11, 1919)

This is true for all aspects of methodology. If in some particular main lesson, for instance, the students use loose pages for a particular main lesson, rather than bound main lesson books, and they are not expected to write anything for the entire main lesson block but instead can decide for themselves what they want to do for the block – that will have a very enlivening effect not only on that main lesson but also on the later ones, too.

When I was in high school, we had a fairly well known teacher of literature. Not only were his lessons extraordinarily compelling, he also knew how to get us to work. In 11th grade he once said to us: "For this main lesson there will be no homework from me. You decide yourself what you want to do." The only task was: every morning we had to write in a notebook, as a sort of collective diary, what we each had done. Before the lesson began he took a look at it, and chose something from which he could launch his lesson. At the end of the block there was an exhibition and display of all our individual efforts. We never worked so hard as for this block.

For reasons I cannot fathom, the notion that the main lesson consists of a rhythmical part ("morning circle") and a working part has spread through the Waldorf schools. I assume that the reason for this idea is that we should "tune" the children in preparation for the lesson, and of course that can happen in a variety of ways. But this notion has taken on a hard-and-fast form; indeed, it has become a yardstick by which to measure Waldorf education generally: the rhythmical part, it is said, belongs to the Waldorf method. That is not true! The idea has become hollow and only the form remains. Then we see how an unjustifiably large part of the main lesson is used for all sorts of exercises, which have nothing at all to do with the subsequent main lesson. And yet, in the middle grades, teachers hang on to this practice; you see the bored faces of the children and write them off as being signs of approaching puberty. In fact, it is really quite a different matter. Such a morning circle isn't appropriate for this age and the children react correctly, for it is a form without any content. They resist. Then comes the so-called "lesson". Now everything which should be present has disappeared: a breathing pulsing between attention and relaxation, a breathing between absorbing and being active, the weaving between seriousness and humor. In this way the sheer form can destroy any pedagogical relevance.

A colleague is about to start teaching a biology main lesson to a 9th grade. He observes the students and notices how little they enjoy thinking. He makes a lightning-fast decision. Every day he will use the first ten minutes of his lesson to present thoughts from Aristotle's' logic. The young people not only respond enthusiastically, but also remain present and inwardly engaged for the entire main lesson block. Pedagogical relevance has been created. We see how the question of relevance reaches beyond the schedule right into the way we form the lessons. It is like the skin of a living body: it has to breathe.

3. The Meaning of Intellect in School

"But what has to be thoroughly understood is that the soul-spiritual does not become intellectual before puberty, that intellect develops naturally only with puberty."
(*The Roots of Education,* GA 309, lecture 4, Bern, April 16, 1924)

Waldorf schools have an image problem. Everything which seems soft in the Waldorf schools, which appears otherworldly and no longer relevant in this day and age, is actually advantageous because it is future-oriented: all learning is steeped in what the entire soul experiences.

But this too is liable to be criticized, because an opinion is abroad that learning is not important in the Waldorf schools, that it is ranked second in importance and that therefore the students don't learn enough. It's an old complaint, which in my opinion may well be true in some cases, but not of the original intentions of a Waldorf school.

What it is going on?

In everything a class is supposed to be able to do, whether it's arithmetic or reading or any other subject, we are always dealing with a reality we can influence and develop only up to a point. A child's innate capacity for understanding can be increased only to a moderate degree. Therefore, in this regard, we are always dealing with a sort of uncertainty in relation to the children, a quiet fear of the incomprehensible.

This leads us back to the idea of the "doability" or efficacy of the lessons: education has achieved its mission, it is said, when each child can do the same thing. There are endless methods to achieve this goal, and some of them are astonishingly ingenious.

However, if we follow this path, we have to admit that the art of education has become the technique of education. The challenge mentioned above, which ought to be the source of inner re-enlivenment, that the path of learning should to be part of the rest of life, will never be met in this way.

The first thing which we as teachers must achieve is the thought that education as an art is a path which, in the long run, promotes, rather than weakens, the children' intelligence. It is essential for us to realize this. This realization goes beyond the efficacy of educational technique; it exists in a spiritual, mental realm, there where it pertains to us as teachers; it exists in the realm on the level of psychology in the anthroposophical sense, in the realm which pertains to the understanding of child development.

A significant help for this is, once again, *Study of Man*. In the 11th lecture, a paradigm shift in education is portrayed that couldn't be more fundamental, assuming a school strives for it. In this lecture we see the three-fold aspect of the human organism, and its three realms: the head spirit, the rhythmical part with the trunk (!), and the limbs. Then we get a description of how the cognitional part (head) cannot be educated, how the middle part of the human being can be only partially educated, and that only the limbs, meaning the will, can be educated. In other words, education should begin with the education of the will and then—via the feelings—awaken the intellect. In Steiner's words: *"All we really have to do is to develop the limb man and part of the chest man. For after that it is the task of the limb man and chest man to awaken the head man. Here we come to <u>the true function of teaching and education</u>."* (emphasis added) The entire situation is summarized in these words: *"The thing we can accomplish best in our* *teaching is the education of the will, and part of the education of the feeling life."* (*Study of Man*, GA 293, lecture 11, Stuttgart, September 2, 1919)

This is presented in a context that is important for today. For what is the teacher's stance if he has students who are intellectually more capable than he is himself? If he were to educate them only through the intellect, these students would progress only as far as the teacher himself had progressed. Untold problems, well known in the realm of education for the gifted, would result. But if the education of the will is an integral part of the teacher's own life, if he is ethically pure in his pedagogical striving, if he is not secretly striving to produce intellectual clones of himself, then we have a key for the education of gifted, and even very gifted youngsters. For the honest will to do what is right will increase in the teacher.

At present, we are experiencing a historical transition, a paradigm shift, in which education ceases to consist of stuffing the student's head. Education is no longer "top down" but "bottom up". In its pure form this motto applies all the way to the sixth or seventh year of school.

Let's try, first of all, to grasp this shift in general terms. In the lower grades, the typically child-appropriate approach posits that the capacity for understanding develops unconsciously in successive stages through practice and repetition. If we assume that capacities of intelligence reside in the etheric body, then we sense the justification of this approach. The soul (astral body) then takes on the role of making things "tasty" for the etheric body, by awakening the joy of learning through love of the teacher and the subject. If that happens, then the children will not suffer under the teacher (which can give rise to the absurd misunderstanding that if joy is present, nothing will be learned). This perception is significant, for it shows that consciousness, in the sense of self-consciousness, is not part of the actual learning process. The "learning body" must, indeed, be educated like a body, rather than like the occupant of a body. It's better not to wear a partly finished coat; it's good neither for the coat nor for the wearer. (This view of the learning process is held against the Waldorf school in a variety of ways. Supposedly it prevents the children from becoming independent, or it staunches their creativity and such, or it supposedly prevents the child from finding his own path of learning. Indeed: here is a parting of the ways.) A child begins to be involved in his own process of learning only after he has begun to think independently, when of himself, for instance, he begins to find connections between ideas. Thus, when he tries to grasp causal connections, he is wearing his "coat of logic" and can apply what he has learned. This awakening of the children, in which they discover themselves as learners, can be noticed from the 6th grade onwards. When that happens, and the conscious soul and "learning body" draw nearer to each other, then the teacher's task is to challenge both in equal measure. This he accomplishes by making sure that in the learning process the soul experiences what the etheric body is learning: namely, through the high art of imaginative teaching. In the years that follow, we see how that which is to be learned connects with consciousness; the student become capable of judgment, meaning, he become capable of deciding to use his own intellect.

If, in the course of the child's development, these processes are confused, it will, generally speaking, be to the detriment of the capacities of intelligence, in relation to the remaining capacities that can and should develop in the child. In this domain, restraint gives rise to strength and ability. Premature advancement depletes strength and ability.

Contemporary culture, however, when it comes to matters of education, is almost dogmatically wed to the phrase: the earlier the better. A fine example can elucidate the value of just the opposite.

One of the greatest violinists of the twentieth century was the Russian virtuoso, David Oistrakh. In his autobiography he describes growing up in Odessa, where he had a violin teacher he revered. This teacher understood the extraordinary talent of his pupil. He undertook the following plan with him. Until he was 20 years old, he let him practice all manner of violin pieces, but not the works of the great musical masters. Only when Oistrakh had mastered all aspects of technique, did his teacher lead him to the greats: Bach, Mozart, Beethoven, Mendelssohn, Brahms, Bruch, Tchaikovsky. Their works he now grasped with incredible inner strength and maturity. Until his (premature) death, Oistrakh was connected in deep gratitude to this teacher for holding him back.

And wasn't it the famous Swiss biologist, Adolf

Portmann, who, already years ago, established that what is characteristic for all animal development is acceleration, whereas what is characteristic for human development is that it restrains itself? (The antithesis of accelerating and retarding development.)

One last extraordinary example may still further elucidate the sentence by Rudolf Steiner quoted above. A remarkable article appeared in a Dutch newspaper. A young man earned five masters degrees from the University of Utrecht in five (!) different subjects. This despite the fact that years earlier in grade school when, at the age of 12, he had to decide which high school specialization he should pursue, the teachers at the time could not agree whether he was even good enough for high school.

4. Class Size and Individualization

Another burning question relates to class size and the fear that individual children will not receive proper attention in a large class. This fear sometimes translates into an actual complaint about the Waldorf schools. It is well known that Rudolf Steiner approved of large classes. How then do we see this? How necessary is it that the elementary school grades (through 8th grade) remain small? Where does this notion originate? It's unclear whether it's the teachers or the parents who fear for the progress of their children. The fact remains that it's a doctrine of our times to aim for individualizing a child's education.

After all, it's commonly accepted that children today are maturing sooner, becoming more independent, more self-aware. There is talk about "new children" who are already adult in childhood. We also hear about "star children" who bring capacities that pose heretofore unaccustomed challenges to educators. Above all, it's the classical "education from the front of the room" which is now thought to bring about exactly what the "new children" don't need.

Here, too, we confront the fact that what used to be strength becomes weakness if it is not thought through and thoroughly structured. The art of education was never meant to be a merely "frontal" education. The possible forms for structuring lessons within a true art of education are limitless. And it is quite clear, that when a teacher is teaching a class, he has to be so intensively present that the children experience: he is there for me.

If I believe that the size of a class will be the essential impediment to reaching individual students, then teaching a class of any size will become an almost unbearable burden. Once this feeling arises, then no matter what the actual size of the class, it will be too big. We must raise ourselves up to the un-ordinary thought that it is just the teaching of (relatively) large classes that produces the proper relationship between the teacher and the students. A child needs to be surrounded by the effect of the group, a child needs the muting and arresting influence of the class community. Now and then the child needs to be unnoticed; now and then the child needs to be able to be invisible in the group and yet still know: my teacher is there for me.

Let us consider the thoughts laid out in the chapter of Steiner's *Theosophy* entitled "Reincarnation and Karma". There we are reminded of a very special reality. All human experience is acquired through the senses, internalized through mental picturing, and transformed by the memory into something permanent for the soul. In this way the experiences that a human being has are spared from being transitory. Instead, experiences can be awakened through the soul again and again, thus providing permanence to what can otherwise become fleeting. Whatever the soul has learned through these experiences, it takes as fruits into life after death.

In the chapter mentioned above, the question then arises: what happens with the retention of human deeds and activities? Remarkably, these do not impress themselves on the soul, they remain apart from us, yes, even apart from my influence. For instance, I take the train, I arrive at the time I thought I would. Do I know all the people who through their professional activity made it possible for me to get from point A to point B punctually? I do not know them, and they do not know me. Someone is a baker, and through his deeds he enables me to work and to accomplish my own deeds, in that I eat his bread each day. I buy a coat that enables me to move about in winter, and also to go to work, because it keeps me warm. I don't know who made it; in turn, the person who made it also doesn't know me, who wears the result of his labor. It is a good exercise, for ourselves but also for our students, to examine a day in our lives and to consider how that day depends on the deeds of other people, even though we don't know many of the people who have contributed to it.

If we do that, we will discover how we are part of a network of deeds and activities, how we are enmeshed in hundreds of relationships. It is a true destiny-network, though at first unconscious. However, a simple consideration will demonstrate that the essential expression of the human being is his deeds, his activity. After all, we write our biography through our deeds. If I encounter someone on the street whom I don't know, I can determine very little through outer appearances. Space gives me only a limited answer. But if I have the opportunity to accompany this human being for a part of his life's path, something of his being will be revealed to me. For that I need to see into the timeline of his life of deeds.

So the essential elements, my deeds, do not reveal themselves to the soul, for they are "invisible" to me; instead, they go out into the world.

It makes no difference whether your deeds are outwardly visible to others (as when, for example, you are an architect and build a house for a grateful client) or invisible (as when you are a mother raising your children, who take her actions completely for granted). Furthermore, you can ask yourself: a human being has lived and died. How is it then with the network of deeds which, hidden, remain behind in the world? Human beings take the fruits of life's experiences with them across the threshold of death. However, on earth, the deeds of life remain. As we saw, they comprise an entire network. We should remember that these deeds are closely connected to the ego of the human being.

This is the network of relationships into which the human being places himself again when he reincarnates. Perhaps we can also say that in doing so there is a "peripheral ego-quality" that we meet here on the earth, and possibly we are justified in imagining that this quality is particularly effective in childhood, when life is determined more from without than from within.

Now we have a basis for understanding why children look for other children with whom to play; that, on the whole, children are eager to visit families where there are many children, that children feel comfortable in communities, feel as if they are wearing a comfortable coat; that children from large families generally find it easier to integrate themselves into the world. For the actual surrounding is one that is inwardly related to all children!

Children have little understanding for the personal, individual path of learning. They embrace the school day as a fact of life, which they experience, above all, with a common consciousness, and which they prefer not to scrutinize individually. Everything to do with consciousness does not come from the child, but is, instead, awakened in the child from without. How appropriately or inappropriately these forces of consciousness are awakened in the child depends on the adults' tactfulness. This brings us back to understanding the merits of having a smaller or larger class. In the final analysis, it's a matter of answering the question: how much consciousness do I awaken in the child at the appropriate, or inappropriate, time? The fewer children there are around the child and therefore the more I as a teacher will engage the child only in an I-you relationship, the more I appeal to the forces of consciousness.

This fact ought to be borne in mind regarding the class size. The larger the community of the class, the more the child will recognize itself in a social environment. This won't happen as a deed of self-recognition, but as an experience of the self in life itself. In addition, the community of the class is the place for practicing sociability.

If now the proper individualization arises within the class community, then we are moving in a sphere that is appropriate for the child. Some examples: a colleague reports how, as a Waldorf pupil in 7th grade, he had his first chemistry main lesson with a very well-known teacher whom he respected highly. They were working on the differences between acids and bases. The teacher did the experiments and all the students watched expectantly and with great interest. Now, twenty years later that former student—by now a teacher himself—has to teach this main lesson. He immediately notices: my students cannot watch and listen the way we did back then. Their capacity for imagination is not strong enough.

He divides the class into five groups, distributes the tasks and gives each group eight substances to taste as to their sourness, bitterness, sweetness, or saltiness. Then the children, following his (written) instructions, place these substances in a test tube, fill it with distilled water, shake it, and add red cabbage juice. They then compare the changes in color with the various tastes and substances, and write all this up themselves. An inspiring experience of the first steps in chemistry is complete. The community has had the experience, but also the children have experienced it individually. (With thanks to my colleague Ruud Gersons for this example.)

Another case: in a 6th grade, the class teacher wants to give a main lesson on language with the very special intention of teaching the students to express something in words as precisely as possible; choice of vocabulary and syntax should be so exact that only one formulation is possible: it must be formulated exactly like this, and no other way. In the classical curriculum the business letter is meant to serve this purpose. But the class teacher has not found a relationship to the business letter. After a long, somewhat despairing search, she is inspired by a walk through the harbor to distribute as many ropes to the class as there are children. Then she teaches them to tie sailors' knots. The children practice and practice until they can tie the various knots. One group learns the double loop bowline, another the flat knot, yet another the anchor hitch, etc. When the children have mastered the various knots, they have to describe the knots and how to make them with such precise instructions that anyone could make the knot by following them. An attempt to carry out the instructions formulated by the students proves whether they were sufficiently correct and precise.

Exact illustrations are added to the verbal description, and the main lesson goes perfectly: common experience through individual striving. (With thanks to my colleague Edith Ploeg.)

Another example: two teachers of parallel 5th grades want to promote better understanding by means of work that both classes could do. They have the idea of creating shell mosaics of various motifs which can be found on historical buildings in the city where the school is located. Since the town is by the sea, the two classes go to the shore in order to collect lots of shells. These are dried, and then large plywood boards are sawed into smaller pieces. Meanwhile, other students have collected the motifs. Their pictures are displayed, and everyone makes the choice together. Meanwhile, yet another group has prepared a powerful cementing glue, and mixed groups of eight, combining students from both classes, get to work. In a few days both classrooms smell a lot like the North Sea. But then the pictures start to evolve, and the joy in the common success grows in each group day by day. When the mosaics are finished, they are painted, and finally they are fixed with hair spray. Joyfully (but carefully, because they are heavy) and triumphantly the mosaics are hung up in the school corridors. Both classes have had a strong, common experience, but each child can be proud of the work. (With thanks to my colleague Harry Gubbels.)

If we experience the value and meaning of the class community, then the appropriate possibilities for individualizing the lesson will arise. Whether you differentiate according to tempo on one occasion, or another time according to degrees of difficulty: if it takes place within the class community it will be socially acceptable, and thus profit the children. Differentiating within the class is a socially acceptable, individualizing process within the class community. However, if you use such differentiation to achieve what you otherwise would not, then you bring something alien into the class that is socially divisive. When the Atelierschule (high school) of the Zürich Steiner School introduced its matriculation program, it could only do that through differentiation within the uppermost grades. The school inspectors, visiting the classes, were unable to determine which students were headed for the matriculation and which were not.

The exams, prepared in this way, were passed successfully by all of the students (communicated by Robert Thomas).

As many people may know, Rudolf Steiner imagined, at the very beginning of the Waldorf School, that foreign language instruction would consist of combined classes divided by levels of ability, so that the large differences in ability could be met. Why could he suggest something so "hard"? (Indeed, the colleagues at that time did not take up the suggestion.) Because he knew that the class community was hale and hearty. This example can show us how far the possibilities of the art of education can be stretched.

5. About the Autonomy of the Teacher

Properly understood, the teacher's autonomy is a matter of independence and the capacity for judgment with respect to the pedagogical activity of the teacher. Many so-called mainstream schools already value such autonomy to a high degree, indeed promote it. Apart from that, the teacher is expected to contribute especially to anything that unifies the school. In so doing, it is the highest form of freedom to have the will to be in harmony with the colleagues, so as to do whatever is beneficial for the school.

That is easy to write, but harder to enact. It is detrimental to a school community if a teacher decides "on pedagogical grounds" to write his reports a year from now, because he doesn't consider it sensible to do it this year.

Nor does it affect a school community positively if a new colleague decides to keep his Saturdays free, while the rest of the school is in session on that day. And it weakens a school community if colleagues decide on their own whether they can or can't participate in faculty meetings. These are crude examples. A more nuanced example of a teacher's autonomy might take place in a school with parallel classes. Can the colleagues agree to a shared curriculum without creating large differences? Do these colleagues agree on common academic end-of-year goals? If one class undertakes a class trip of more than a week, will it be possible to arrange for the colleague of the other class to do something similar?

If a colleague is good at rehearsing class plays throughout the years, and if his colleague in a parallel class is new and has no experience in that realm, will there be collegial cooperation? (The habit of doing something really big only in the 8th grade—which usually exhausts the capacity of the 8th graders and upsets the school routine for weeks, and then forces the classes that follow to accomplish something even greater—need not be discussed further since it has already been addressed in an earlier chapter. Staging something smaller more frequently is more effective and might even be pedagogically better, as already mentioned.)

The real autonomy of the teacher lies in a different realm. It exists wherever the human being in general, and the teacher more specifically, remains a learner. This autonomy exists in the realm of inner activity.

A quick look at the soul-spiritual dynamic of development is appropriate here. How does the human being develop over time? Is the human being of today the same as he or she was 200 or 400 years ago? Rudolf Steiner provides important indications concerning these questions, indications which are especially meaningful for the pedagogue, even if they were not given in a pedagogical context.

In various places he describes how the human capacities for development are subject to dynamic processes. Let us bring to mind how incredibly strong the capacity for learning is in the human being during the first 14 years of life. We need to realize that in earlier times this capacity for development and learning used to continue over almost the entire span of a human life. More recently, this capacity has declined. According to Steiner, the natural capacity for human development now continue until the 27th or 28th year of life.

After that the human being, as a natural being, must be satisfied with what he has achieved. Further development can come about only through his "ego" and not through natural development. (See among other references: *A Social Basis for Primary and Secondary Education*, GA 192, lecture 11, Stuttgart, June 29, 1919 and, *The Renewal of Education*, GA 301, lecture 4, Basel, April 23, 1920.)

Alongside this indication, I would like to place a second, also by Steiner. Coinciding more or less with this "rejuvenation of humanity" something else has changed, namely, the configuration of our sleep.

Here is the quotation:

"For instance, it can never be said of a growing child that the ego and astral body plunge fully into the physical and etheric bodies, and become completely one with them as regards activity. And if we look back into earlier times of human evolution, to the important dividing line which occurs in the middle of the 15th century, we must admit that until that definite point in human life as a whole, there existed no complete immersion of the ego and astral body during conscious waking hours. The momentous significance in our post-Atlantean age is that soul and spirit - our ego and astral body - have only recently been able to plunge entirely into the physical and astral bodies, and even now, not until after the 27th or 28th year. Conditions will change somewhat again with time.

This is a significant mystery in the evolution of mankind. Only now can the human being experience a full immersion into his physical body, but only after having reached full maturity at age 27 or 28.

What is the meaning of this complete immersion into the physical body? It signifies that we are thereby able to develop thoughts and unfold ideas of the materialistic, natural/scientific type, prevalent since the days of Galileo and Copernicus. For these ideas and this natural/scientific view of the world, the physical body is the right instrument. This identification had not been achieved in earlier centuries. Therefore, there existed no natural/scientific thinking wholly bound up with the physical body."

Further along we read:

"In the present time, much must be made anew, whereby what I mean by "present time" is, of course, an extended period of time. Above all, things such as the goals of education must become new."

And in conclusion, in the same lecture, Steiner says:

"Anyone observing life today knows that in our time there live an uncommonly large number of people who cannot come to terms with life. Why is this? Because - as described earlier - they cannot look back to childhood events and experiences essential in their upbringing and education. Certain forces can only be developed in childhood. When this is the case, they are ours for life, and we are able to cope with events. If we have not acquired these forces, we cannot cope with life.

It is in this sense that we must understand the feeling of responsibility, which must be acquired with respect to

everything connected to child-rearing and education."
(*The Problem of Our Time*, GA 193, lecture 8, Berlin,
September 14, 1919)

We now understand why Rudolf Steiner draws our
attention, again and again, to the fact that the task of a
new education is to concern itself with the capacity for
self-development in old age, even though we see that
today the polarity between youth and age has never
been greater. (*The Problem of Our Time*, GA 193, lecture 7, Berlin, September 13, 1919; GA 193, lecture 3,
Zurich, February 11, 1919)

Is it possible for us as educators to dedicate ourselves to this task? But first we need to consider something else. How do I myself stand in this world? What
is the state of my own youth forces, and what is my
own "broken nature"? Here is not the place for fatal-
ism. Every human being can change himself once he
recognizes himself in his own being. For this to happen, however, a path of self-knowledge is required.
For some, self-knowledge arises through a crisis. But
it needs to be mentioned that a path to self-knowledge
can also be found without a crisis.

Finding the path to self-knowledge cannot be taken
for granted, especially because the phrase is current,
without deeper understanding. Here is a possible approach: Imagine that we are pursuing our daily work.
What do we experience in ourselves? At work we experience a particular success. We ask ourselves: how did
this actually happen? Is it my own accomplishment,
for example because I really prepared well for this
task? That may be. But it can also be the case that I suc-

ceed in something and yet have to admit that I, myself, contributed nothing, or very little, to it: it happened as if by itself.

Or: We experience a failure at work. I can ask myself how this happened. Perhaps my preparations were inadequate. In that case the situation is clear. But it can also happen that I prepared very thoroughly and still failed. Well, in the latter case it's customary to blame difficult circumstances. This is not a fruitful path for the pedagogue. Better that we seek the cause of failure in ourselves. Then we'll see that we are often incapable of judging in this realm. We experience—both positively as well as negatively—that there seems to be something else that is at work here. What is that? It must have something to do with me. In this way it becomes possible to develop a feeling for a "second" person in me, someone who is not outwardly visible. Simply becoming aware of this fact works wonders for achieving self-knowledge. We get to know our abilities and our limitations. We begin to notice the places in ourselves that, in relationship to the world of deeds, require care and work. In addition, we begin to acquire a sense for our actual intentions of what we want to become in the future.

If you attempt to do this, you will discover that you become less dependent, less sensitive and vulnerable vis-à-vis the world at large. You will have initiated a new self-confidence.

The autonomy of the teacher actually lies in such inner realizations. If you keep yourself mobile, practice being someone who is continually in development, you will also find the proper relationship to your circumstances. Such is the path of the inner human being, which for the teaching profession, simply stated, turns out to be a requirement, if you are to be effective in that work.

Merely being on that path and then becoming involved in teaching can fill you with an overwhelming experience of gratitude for your life. You may experience how, for a time, you are in balance with yourself and your tasks. It is truly an experience that is hardly comparable with anything else. You experience a profound gratitude for being allowed to practice this profession. And gratitude can only be present for what happens to me, not for what "I" achieve.

10. SOMETHING ABOUT CHILD STUDY

A twelve-year-old girl is described at a faculty meeting. She was delicately built, a graceful girl. Already the photo of her from her first school year shows, for example with respect to her visage, that everything had the tendency to be finely formed. This girl was a good learner; in her behavior she tended to be a bit formal and stiff; she was pleasant in her interactions with the other children, but not always socially adept; she distinguished herself by having an extraordinary gift for drawing.

Starting in the first grade, she was capable of drawing human figures in unerring outline, similar to what we know from Walt Disney characters. All her illustrations for the school presentations (fairy tales, legends, bible stories, Norse mythology) had this style. Her ability intensified to the point where she could, with a single stroke, portray a look, facial expression, or posture so brilliantly that one could discern in her a genuine talent.

But the curious thing was, that this ability simply disappeared if a landscape or tree or river was to be portrayed. Then her drawings were clumsy, as if drawn by someone else. When asked to participate in a drawing contest, she declined. As mentioned, this girl learned easily, but with a tendency toward perfectionism; if she suspected that her efforts were not going to result in perfection, she wouldn't even tackle the task.

Something else was notable. She had only partial control over her metabolism. She suffered so strongly from flatulence that at times the space surrounding her had to be practically cleared. This was the case leading up to the time of the study, and the faculty felt pretty helpless about her situation.

The question now was: can we understand this girl as she appears?

We tried to come to an integrated view of what had been presented. We asked ourselves, can it be that her somewhat formal appearance, the formality of her language, and her specialized talent for drawing are all symptoms of one and the same condition? Can it be that a strong, possibly overly strong life in the imagination is being expressed? A life so strongly imagined that the courage needed to try something fails her unless she can feel completely certainty about it? Might it be that this powerful imaginative life, which has connected itself actively only to the realm of drawing, has, in part, prevented her metabolism from connecting to the organism as a whole, so that the will is alien to it? After all, a metabolism that provokes too much flatulence is a sign the astral body is insufficiently engaged in the metabolism, which is just the realm where the astral body should be especially concentrated.

Light and Warmth

If we want to educate human beings appropriately, we need to integrate warmth and light processes through enthusiasm and feelings engendered by the lesson. With this girl, the impression arose that in her light was very little connected with warmth. How to bring them together? It seemed that it would be just before puberty that the possibility of integrating "above" with "below" would be significant. It became apparent that the capacity of imagination was strong, but the middle sphere was rather insecure, and the lower aspects were only partially engaged.

The question arose: assuming we take this as the working hypothesis, how can we help the child?

Whenever we are dealing with something that is within the parameters of what is normal, we are entitled to ask whether it's possible to be actively helpful through the teaching itself. Someone suggested that this girl should have extra sessions of wet-on-wet painting, in order to offset her strong tendency to create rigid forms. This suggestion was quickly set aside, for whenever you want to help someone, you have to start with what they know and can do. At least initially painting wet-on-wet would be too big a jump for her constitution. Instead it was agreed that the girl (who was about to enter 5th grade) would start with free-hand geometry and extra sessions in form drawing. We also agreed to ask a drawing teacher from the art academy to assess whether indeed she did have a special talent, and if so, how she could be helped to overcome her tendency to draw in fixed linear ways.

Now it was also necessary to interest her metabolism in the life of imagination, so that these two aspects of her being could relate more easily to each other. The impression arose that pedagogy alone would not suffice. There was no school doctor at this school. So we were left to our own resources. We tried to get closer to the question of warmth. Where does warmth originate? Through the combination of the powers of recognition and interest. In the elementary school, however, the opposite process holds true: first interest, enthusiasm, doing, then learning (as described by Steiner in lecture 11 of *Study of Man*); in this way one awakens the forces of cognition. The class teacher attempted to avoid "academic" instruction, and instead followed this basic rule of education as much as possible. Because there was no therapeutic eurythmist at this school, not much could be attempted in that realm.

The parents were asked to give the girl a warm, sweet breakfast, and to take care that in the evening a copper ointment be applied to her belly or some warm clothing provided for additional warmth.

After all these directives, it was agreed to return to this child study in eight weeks with two questions: did we do what we decided to do, and did it help? The results of this case are not yet available because this study was initiated only a short time ago. Nevertheless, the description shows us how, when concerning themselves with the being of a student, the faculty can make headway in coming to understand a particular. Thus, by coming to an inner experience of the being of the child we find the strength to help.

Three Steps

The child study is a collective achievement of the faculty. It does not need any particular method. Still, anyone can notice that it will proceed, as if on its own, through three steps.

In the first step, an attempt is made to compose a portrait of the student. How has the student developed over time? How does the student take hold of space? What can we learn from this? Many phenomenological examples are offered and the circle of colleagues tries to discern the symptoms from out of the phenomena; is what I am hearing specific to this child? Often, insignificant things are mentioned, and then all of a sudden, something is said that is perplexing; something that is special, something one ought to remember. The class teacher depicts the student, also outlines the reasons why this student is being discussed; the picture is then supplemented by contributions from the colleagues. It is not necessary to carry out this first step exhaustively. True, we may wish to linger on this step, since it is the only one in which we can rely on our experience and our understanding. It's good, however, if the discussion leader (preferably not the class teacher or class mentor of the student under discussion) interrupts the gathering of examples after a given period of time, once the picture is complete enough, so that the next step can be attempted.

Before we describe this next step, one other thing needs to be mentioned. It's precisely this first step of the child study that requires the following capacity: the portrayals should not be affected by the sympathies or antipathies of the teachers. Also, a particular "coloring" can slip in, whenever the students of a certain teacher are presented ("his students are always like that, obviously"). Also, there must not be the slightest mood of judgment about a student. If such moods arise, do what you may, the being of the student will disappear from the circle of colleagues, and the study becomes meaningless. The first step, even if it is the simplest of the three steps, determines whether a genuine discussion will take place or not. A relatively strong soul-hygiene is required of the participants. If it succeeds, then the step to the second part will be expected; all will want to proceed in search of the being of the student …

As the picture is filled in, we have to ask ourselves whether we understand what we have heard and seen. Can we penetrate beyond the sensory information to an understanding of the causes and connections? Just as the first step correlates to a case history, so the second step correlates to a diagnosis. You can only find the proper remedies in the third step, if you first know what you're dealing with.

Which capacities are needed for this second step? I will indicate three. First of all, you need some expertise in the realm of anthroposophical anthropology, just as expertise is the basis of any profession. In addition, you are dependent on the knowledge of others. The child study gets its strength from the common striving of the faculty. This process becomes effective through the circle of teachers. Only then will content arise. The third aspect I'd like to mention here is the fact that it is not only the knowledge of the human being which get us further. What is also needed is a sense for connections, for relationships. That arises not only through logical conclusions, but requires a certain feeling capacity. In the 6th lecture of *Study of Man*, we find the well-known drawing in which Steiner represents three steps in the process of cognition: "wakeful pictorial cognition", "dreaming inspired feeling", "sleeping intuitive willing". In this second part of the child study we find ourselves in the second step of "inspired feeling". This means the sense of certainty of the foundations that accompanies the first basic step, the pictorial cognition, has been left behind.

As we saw in the example, we no longer find ourselves on solid ground of sense perception. Rather perception on a different level must be practiced. And indeed, in child study, a lot depends on practice. The entirety of *Study of Man* is the background, the "grammar" for our understanding. Thus, in addition to the four temperaments, which Steiner offers to elucidate an understanding of the developing human being, there are other perspectives:

1. the polarity of large headed – small headed (which has more to do with the child's particular manner of thinking than with the size of the head)
2. the polarity of fantasy rich – fantasy poor (which concerns itself with the independence of the power of imagination)
3. the polarity of cosmic – earthly (whereby the main directions of interest in the soul are recognized)

4. the polarity of an ego too deeply or too loosely connected with the physical body.

In addition there are the observations about the way the etheric body, the astral body, and ego organization can be perceived. Steiner's point of departure is that the developing human being is so transparent that these "bodies" express themselves visibly. Experience teaches us that determining the constitution of the etheric body (or the body of formative forces, or the learning body) often provides a very useful portal for the second part of the child study. This body expresses itself in the capacity to take something in, to retain it, to form it, and to give it structure (for example, when writing or drawing).

All these perspectives culminate in the question of the relationship of the upper human being with the lower, as expressed in the first lecture of *Study of Man:* "The task of education conceived in the spiritual sense is to bring the Soul-Spirit into harmony with the Life-Body."

Then you can perceive the stream of time: how does the young person develop from birth onward? What is his relationship to his body, which illnesses arose and when, or was this child always healthy?

How can we arrive at certainty in the face of such questions?

If our first step was an attempt to find the way from phenomenon to symptom, then what we are looking for here are experiences of evidence from the circle of colleagues. Can we confirm that what is presented is consistent with the being of the child? You can notice how the conversations become more intimate when they are true. Anyone can notice this: is intimacy present or not?

We can fall into the trap of "psychologizing", which is a risk at this level: namely, the tendency to interpret everything psychologically. If this happens, the being of the child will seem to draw back, and we enter a peculiar sphere of illusory rationality.

This step also does not need to be taken to completion. Perhaps enough has been gathered for the discussion leader to suggest that we now consider how to help the child.

If the second step required a sort of soul courage, we are now asked to become engaged with our will.

You will find the path toward help only if you really awaken in yourself the will to seek help, even if you are a colleague who has never even worked with the child in question. No matter, it is still, in one respect, a matter of this will. How then do we arrive at an answer? If we take as our point of departure the idea that a true art of education must have a healing effect, then we must find this healing in the subject matter of the lessons and in the manner of the teaching.

This means the faculty needs to acquire some rudimentary knowledge of how the curriculum affects the student. How does arithmetic affect the student? Reading? Drawing? Singing? Grammar? What do these subjects bring about in the various sheaths of the student? How do they contribute to the forming of the student?

This is not a matter of theory. What we need to know is how the lesson affects the student: does the lesson cause fatigue or does it invigorate, does the student become warmer or colder? That already tells us a lot. Many colleagues have transformed such experiences into a kind of teaching instinct; they know: this can follow after that, this not, and so forth.

In a normal situation we look for a way to help, using the lesson itself. Only in the case of a special need do we seek help from beyond the realm of pedagogy itself.

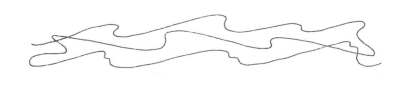

11. Healing Forces in the Life with the Children and Students, or How to Find Active Equanimity

As we have already noted, teaching, nowadays, for a variety of circumstances, is no longer an easy profession.

Some of the causes are societal: stress due to lack of time, complicated life circumstances, the organizational needs of a school organism, high demands, lofty expectations, the social fabric, lack of adequate income. Other causes arise from the personal sphere.

In considering the latter category, we have to recognize the fact that not every teacher can look back on a joyful school time. The following exercise will demonstrate how significant this is.

Without giving it too much thought, recall something from your own time at school. Whatever you remember, one thing is certain, the memories will come quickly; little contemplation is necessary, and you do not need to reach down into deep wells of memory. The memories lie just beneath the surface of consciousness, they are not far away. Thus it does not require a great leap of thought to realize that even if such memories lie far back in time, they nevertheless continue to color daily life. Is their basic mood sunny or cloudy? It would be good to determine that for yourself. Memories, even if they lie dormant for years, are still there. It's important to clarify for yourself, how they color your own soul. Memories are deeply united with our own ego; the soul aspect thereof colors our fundamental mood of life. Once you've tried this in a general way, separate the memories of your elementary school years from those of your high school years. Is a difference noticeable? These are the phases of human life when the etheric body is first "ego-ized", and then the soul body is "ego-ized". Where are the personal stress points?

(Charles Dickens exemplified this in an incomparably beautiful way in the last of his Christmas Carols. Few know that Dickens wrote four such "songs". Because the first became world famous, the others remained obscure. But it is just the last song, "The Haunted Man", which is especially beautiful. It portrays what happens to a man who, through a seductive spirit, loses all the difficult memories of his youth, because of a so-called "good intention". By losing this memory trove, however, he undergoes horrible changes in character. Luckily, though, it is a Christmas story, and so, at the right moment, all is saved through the love of a girl. Result: "Lord, keep my memory green!")

In short, the coloration, the tone of our own school memories is not always helpful if we have resolved to become teachers. How easily a pessimistic tone, of which you are not even conscious, can reside in the soul's foundation. Yet it is just these unconscious elements that work themselves out in your professional activities, and that is a reason for becoming conscious of your own moods.

Another reality is the environment. What is my relationship to a class, what is my comportment? Am I satisfied and in harmony with the world if the students do exactly what I tell them to do, or what I want them to do, or what I intend for them to do? Or can I also bear it when children just don't do what I intend? Can I keep my balance when the students are naughty, inattentive, and such like? Indeed, can I remain in the same soul state if all about me my intentions and expectations are not being met? How often do I get upset, lose my temper? Am I aware of it myself, or am I already so far gone that I hardly notice it?

If you are satisfied only when the students are "good", you will always be stressed. How long can I stand it? If once you have become used to this attitude, you'll be in danger of wanting to dominate your students willfully. Subsurface stress will hold sway in the class overall, no matter how fine everything appears to be on the surface. We often notice that classes which are carried in this way use the track classes (or subject lessons, as they are also called), to "breathe out". This in turn causes other problems. The first thing for which a new teacher should strive, is a truly sunny disposition that can remain sunny regardless of the classroom situation. Being "good" is not an end in itself!

An example: A 5th grade teacher has decided to do everything possible to teach the children something about grammar. The children, however, simply don't get it. They are full of good will, but, alas, they just don't understand it. The teacher almost despairs. She decides at short notice happily to change the topic, and to let the children forget about the whole thing. She'll try again during the next main lesson. Such a decision is perhaps not rational, but courageous. She rescues the mood, and who knows what the next main lesson may bring. There's no point in weighing down the students with a moral tone about their lack of understanding.

Another example, this time from a 7th grade. Again grammar. A group of girls has "decided" that they just don't want to grasp it. ("Why should we learn this?") If you don't watch out, you will be tempted to turn such a moment into a trial of strength, or you may fall into the judgment that, well, they're just plain stupid. But it's also possible that—in agreement with the parents—you say: "We'll have tea together five times after the lessons, and have as pleasant a time as we can, and at the same time we'll see whether we can't manage it after all." And lo and behold, in the relaxed mood after school, it happens almost naturally that the points of grammar are understood to the point that they become second nature. The only problem when the five pleasant after-school hours are over: the students don't want to give up the privilege …

It's normal that students' inabilities lead to nervousness on the part of the teacher. It would be good to foresee this danger, so that this mood of soul doesn't even arise. Nevertheless, the latent pressure resulting from the fear that the children won't master what they are supposed to learn can pose a real threat to the mood of the lesson, and thus also to the quality of the lesson: Teachers beware!

All these things are seemingly unimportant details. But within these small events in the life of the class there lies much that contributes to the health of the class community and the health of the teacher.

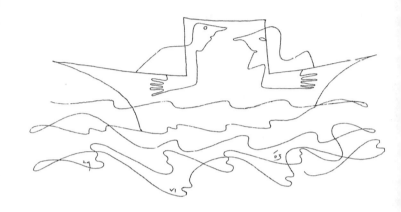

12. Punishment, or the Opportunity for Originality

Another thing that contributes to the healthy atmosphere in a classroom community is the way the teacher handles punishment. How we handle punishment is an important indication of self-knowledge, of how we relate to the class, of how we live with the realities of the classroom. It's well known that naughtiness in the children awakens our displeasure. That is the first trap into which a teacher can blunder.

The teacher ought to avoid being affected in his soul by a punishable deed; he ought to remain free of it. That's easier said than done, and yet in the end it is not so difficult after all. To succeed, it's necessary to hold fast absolutely to Steiner's fundamental indication: we judge the deed, but not the doer (after all, they are children). In addition we should try to think up something original in determining atonement. Anything original has a redemptive effect. If we succeed in avoiding formulas like having the student copy a text, or stay late, or leave the classroom, we will contribute a great deal to the vitality of the class. This is a realm where you can test your own imaginative capacities directly. An example:

A 5th grade is overcome by an epidemic of chewing gum. The teacher asks himself what he should do. He delves into the phenomenon and discovers the following: if you chew gum, everything necessary for digestion is stimulated in the mouth. Saliva is secreted. Not only in the mouth but also in the stomach, secretions take place to prepare for the nourishment to come. But, as we know, no nourishment is forthcoming. So he tells his students the following:

"Listen, dear children. Just imagine you are at home, waiting for a friend. Not only do you want to play together, but your friend is also invited to stay for dinner. Your mother prepares an especially delicious meal. Something special is cooked with a great deal of love. Everything is ready for the visitor. But now something happens. The friend doesn't show up. Doesn't even phone to excuse him or herself. Just doesn't come. How do you feel then? A bit hollow, right? Perhaps even a bit cheated. Well, that is what your stomach feels when you chew gum." Whether the epidemic is allayed by this story is not even that important. The story has revealed the morality of the situation. Well, in this case the chewing gum habit continued. The teacher checked the ingredients of a pack of chewing gum and noticed quite a collection of chemicals listed under "contents". Then he had another idea. To the children he said: "If I catch you chewing gum during class, you'll have to memorize the contents of the package by tomorrow." Then he read out the entire list of ingredients. This did, indeed, do the trick.

Another example: A 9th grader (a boy, of course), behaved quite impossibly during eurythmy. The teacher's patience ran out and she said to him: "Have you any idea how hard it is to teach eurythmy? Next time you'll teach exactly half the lesson. You will teach eurythmy for exactly 25 minutes!" It was an incredible, unforgettable eurythmy lesson. From that time onward, the student was engaged and full of respect for the teacher.

The discovery of misbehavior can even lead to progress in a student and a class, to a real breakthrough. But that will happen only if the teacher keeps a cool head. Indirectly, a teacher finds out that a student has, more than once, taken something from a local store. The teacher takes him aside and quizzes him. After some hesitation, the student confesses. The teacher goes to the store and talks to the owner. They arrive at an agreement whereby the boy will help in the store for several afternoons. After he has overcome his shame, the boy helps out at the store and a heartfelt relationship unfolds between the "sinner" and the store owner ("I, too, was once young."). You will often discover that in cases like this a supportive, mediating conversation with the parents is necessary to prevent unnecessary pressure on the child. Punishment as revenge and expiation is an antiquated concept in the new paradigm of education as given in the art of education. In pedagogical situations, it should be replaced by opportunity. Then punishment reveals itself as the opportunity to transform something that cannot unfold properly. "Punishing" then becomes an opportunity for the teacher, as well, to be pedagogically creative. If a 10th grader is caught smoking in school and it's against the rule, what should be done? You could (as decreed by the school rules) give him a warning, send a letter to the parents ... in short, do the usual thing according to code.

But the teacher can also do the following: "In two weeks you will give a lecture (with black board illustrations) in my class on the plant Nicotiana, what it looks like, how it grows, and its effectiveness as a medicinal plant."

Such a "punishment" does not sour the soul. And the student, to whom this happened, will, for the rest of his life, recall this incident with delight.

Similarly, a young lady in the preparatory class for the Abitur (see glossary) didn't know the answer to a simple problem, whereupon the teacher—without scolding—threatened that if she did not come up with the answer in 30 seconds, he, the teacher, would eat this piece of chalk. She did not come up a solution, and he did eat the chalk, much to the amusement of all present. Then he explained to her in utter calmness how to free herself from such a mental freeze-up.

Such situations make school life worthy of remembering.

From the sphere of "resilience research" we know the importance of having positive memories of school.

13. Temperament, or a View in the Mirror

There's a lot of talk about children's temperament, and rightly so, for grasping the temperament is for the quality of life in the classroom what air is for breathing; either the air is "free" and we understand one another or we feel as if pressed against an invisible and impenetrable wall. Here knowledge of our own temperament as well as our capacity to change our semi-conscious habits play major roles. They are just as significant as the students' temperaments. Do I know my own temperament? Everyone has, at one time or another, been part of a faculty meeting conversation about a class. The teacher excitedly portrays his class as choleric. For the listener, however, the suspicion dawns gradually: Dear Colleague, you're talking about yourself.

One ought to know one's own temperament, and to balance its one-sidedness. How do I determine my own temperament? There are many ways to do that. You might, first of all, visualize your own shape: what does it tell you? Are you tall and thin, or more on the stout side? How do you manage your own weight? Does it take care of itself, or do you have to overcome your own tendency to gain weight? You can ask yourself (and this also works for determining the temperaments of the children): which one am I definitely not? What does my handwriting look like, is it casual and loose, or tight? Is it big or small, angular or round? By these simple means, quite some progress can be made. A subtler way is to visualize how colleagues and parents react to you. Do difficulties in understanding always arise around the same issue?

In considering a grown-up, you should keep in mind that the basic temperament expresses itself differently in thinking, feeling, and willing. It's possible for someone to be quite choleric in his will life, have a definite sanguine tone in his thinking, while having a melancholic mood in his feelings. A tall, thin, graceful colleague who is sanguine through and through may well be strongly choleric in his thinking. A "monochromatic" temperament is rare in adults, whereas a dominant temperament is entirely normal.

Related to the subject of your own temperament is another question you can ask yourself: how inwardly flexible am I? Am I able, when encountering a student, to converse in such a way that I adjust to his temperament empathetically, without pretense? Being able to do that brings about two results: the child, or student, feels understood; and objectivity promotes understanding. If I tell a melancholic child, "Come on now, be happy!" nothing will happen. Inner flexibility is a great virtue when it comes to coexistence with the community of students (not that indifference or superficiality should hold sway). How can we achieve this? The following self-examination can help: how strongly am I imprisoned by my habits? If something interferes with my habit life, does that almost make me ill? Or is it my habit to avoid all habits?

Everyone senses that a teacher who is like a weather vane will have just as much trouble with the community of children as one who clings with an iron will to his own habits and ideas. Let us look at the life of habits from the perspective of *Study of Man*. Habits "live" in the etheric body. This body of formative forces is only partly accessible to the ego and our consciousness, which manifests in our thinking. But it is also partly inaccessible to ego and consciousness. These latter aspects include our life tasks, which are handled autonomously by the etheric body. Located between these two, in a transitional condition, lie our daily habits, which can be made accessible to our consciousness, but not of their own accord. The ego has to be strongly engaged to raise them to consciousness. That is why we find it so difficult to change a habit. For some temperaments, it's almost impossible. So when you try to change some habit or other, you are working on your inner flexibility. And in this regard you can observe that the more modest and realistic your initial attempts, the greater the effect. The result: you will feel refreshed and energized. The ego has reached a part of the body which, until now, it has rarely noticed. (Steiner pointed this out on many occasions, e.g. in the lecture "Overcoming Nervousness" in *Anthroposophy in Everyday Life*, GA 143, January 11, 1912.)

How Long Should a Class Teacher Teach?

From the start, the Waldorf School was organized in such a way that the class teacher would stay with the class for eight years, until the students transitioned into high school. At first this was taken for granted, although it is difficult to find a clear statement on this point in Steiner's pedagogical works. Two short comments are presented here, as examples. The first is notable because the formulation is not prescriptive: *"Nothing is more useful and practical in teaching than if you give the child of 7 or 8 something pictorial, later, perhaps when it is 13 or 14, come back to it in some form or other. Just this is the reason why we, in the Waldorf schools, prefer to keep the child with one teacher for as long as possible. When the children start school at age seven, they are handed over to a teacher. This teacher then proceeds with the children for as long as possible."* (*The Kingdom of Childhood*, GA 311, lecture 4, Torquay, August 15, 1924)

At the end of lecture 11 in *Study of Man*, mention is made of how the teacher can balance any one-sidednesses in a class community with an overview that embraces the entirety of the school years.

"You see, that is why it is so important to keep the children right through their school life; why it is such a mad arrangement to pass the children on to another teacher every year."

Today this practice can no longer be taken for granted. Thus the question must be asked: is it still generally applicable? (We will disregard the obvious, oft heard complaints: what happens if the teacher does not like a child in his class or if the child no longer likes the teacher? For it belongs to the basic professional development of the teacher that he find an appropriate relationship to every student.)

Concerning the length of time a class teacher ought to remain with a class, the following considerations may be helpful: Obviously this wish of Steiner has various levels. One of the most important is this: that the teacher, by accompanying the development of the students through many years, also develops himself. That guarantees that for the teacher, too, the lesson is always new, according to the subject at hand, as well as to the situation. In other words, the teacher also grows. He develops in his capacities not only through the changing subject matter, he actually changes himself; for a 1st grade requires an entirely different posture from a 4th, 6th, or 8th grade.

For the children, this unconscious experience of the teacher's capacity for transformation is of the utmost significance. Consider, for example, how the tone with which the teacher handles the children has to change as they get older. Consider how you meet 6th graders, and how different that was a mere two years ago, when they were still in the 4th grade.

It is this capacity for self-transformation that we need to examine.

When, in the 7th and 8th grades, things "just don't work anymore", it is, generally speaking, more a matter of an insufficient capacity for transformation than insufficient "competence". What is meant by competence is generally considered competence in the subject matter. The necessary knowledge about the subject matter grows with the years, but it wears the cloak of general knowledge, not specific, professional knowledge.

The issue of the teacher possessing adequate conceptual knowledge for the middle school years is in reality a question about the teacher's capacity for transformation. For it is just in the so-called middle school years that we should avoid the trap of instructing the children according to the abstract rules of the subject matter. This is the age when the pedagogical tracks toward puberty are laid. Steiner's pedagogical statements for this age are quite unequivocal:

"Thus, just as the power to write and read is an expression of the teething of the soul, so all activity of imagination, all that is permeated with inner warmth is an expression of what the soul develops in the later school years, the twelfth, thirteenth, fourteenth and fifteenth years. (...) **It is to this power of imagination that we must especially appeal in the latter part of the period between the change of teeth and puberty. We are much more justified in encouraging the child of seven to develop its own intellectuality by way of reading and writing than we are justified in neglecting to bring imagination continually into the growing power of judgment of the child of twelve. For it is from the age of twelve onwards that the power of judgment gradually develops.** (emphasis added) *The teacher must keep alive all his subjects, steep them in imagination. The only way to do this is to permeate all that he has to teach with a*

willing rich in feeling. (...) A thing of the very greatest
importance, a thing to be particularly cultivated during
the later primary school years is the mutual intercourse,
the complete harmony of life, between teacher and chil-
dren."

In my view, this is the only place where Steiner com-
bines what he calls the pedagogical imperative—"keep
your imagination alive"—with a clear statement that
whoever is not ready to develop this capacity should
find a different profession. (*Study of Man,* GA 293,
lecture 14)

The pedagogical earnestness, specifically the pedagogy in relation to the middle school, is thereby characterized.

Perhaps this remark corresponds to the demand
that, rightly understood, imaginative activity must be
grasped and realized anew. But in imaginative activity
there resides a quality closely related to the capacity for
transformation. If we now take a look at the contrast
between the lower and middle grades, then we can see
the entire spectrum of the class teacher's work. Anyone
wanting to achieve this spectrum must transform, must
change himself along with the students.

This raises a remarkable fact: In the realm of eco-
nomics, in industry, in the professional world generally,
there is a lot of talk about flexibility. Flexibility is considered to be one of the most important requirements,
along with sociability. It's important to be able to
master changes, reorganization, new tasks. The same
job for life exists no longer. It's necessary to continually change and adapt. At the same time, however, we

know how hard that is. Unless you are endowed with an exceptionally sanguine nature, you will have a hard time with all this flexibility and change. Where, in fact, does it come from?

Rudolf Steiner characterizes the etheric body, among other ways, as the body of habits. Without an established foundation of acquired habits, we would hardly be able to master our lives. Everyone needs habitual actions, has, in the course of his life, acquired certain habits of feeling and especially habits of thought and of speech. The question then is: how hard and fast are they? Do we recognize them in ourselves? Can we look impartially at our habits? Can we, if we do this, change a habit? Here we approach a significant chapter in the realm of self-education, which can, especially for the teacher, signify success or tragedy in dealing with the changing youngsters. For someone can be a good teacher, but if he does not change his habits along with the naturally changing children, the teachings will suddenly "not work anymore". The previously functioning symbiosis with the class doesn't function anymore, and the teacher has no idea what's wrong. He doubts himself, and runs the danger of hardening something in his soul and beginning to blame his circumstances. The teacher would like to understand what is happening, but cannot find the cause in himself.

A teacher can be exposed to this danger of an insufficient capacity for transformation simply in the habitual way he speaks to the class. If, in the morning, a teacher greets the children in the 4th grade the way he did in the 1st and 2nd grade, he fixes habits in himself and in the class that binds rather than free. The subject teachers are then the first to experience this: they cannot get anywhere with such a class; they have a hard time with the children: the assertion of the children's habits is like a barrier which is hard to overcome.

It is truly a complicated realm. For, of course, a class teacher must build up "good habits" in the class. But not those which create dependencies. How do we determine the difference? The difference lies in this: are the habits which the class teacher works up such that he desires them in freedom, or are they his own, unconscious habits which he needs, above all, to steady himself. Often this distinction is barely perceptible from the outside, but, indeed, all the more potent in effect.

The habit body, the etheric body, has a particular degree of flexibility according to temperament, constitution, and education. This flexibility reveals itself in the soul forces of thinking, feeling, and willing and in their expression. Surely we won't go astray if we assume that today's life circumstances tend to limit the etheric body in its flexibility. You can test this for yourself, by, for example, observing whether you are dependent, during the lesson, on having everything take place the way you planned it. If a "disturbance" arises, are you flustered, or can you be flexible enough to deal with it? It is possible to conclude that this matter of flexibility is the deciding realm in relation to the teacher's durability? If the teacher cannot transform himself along with the students, a sort of "hole" will result in his relation to them. All involved will notice this. Often the hole is then filled with higher academic demands. One advances toward high school pedagogy just as the students are at the age when they depend on an integrated education. We lay the tracks, and with great consequences.

How can we acquire flexibility? Art can be a great teacher in this regard. All artistic activity, also in the classroom, strengthens and supports the etheric body. Another realm of help comes through the particular way of thinking which concerns itself with spiritual scientific (anthroposophical) thought content. This especially promotes flexibility in thinking, as has already been mentioned. It nevertheless remains a difficult practice.

For that reason, let's recall Steiner's remark, "as long as it is possible". Let's take another look at the sentence and imagine it as an "ideal case". Imagine that sometime during 6th grade, a teacher notices that teaching requires more and more effort, things just don't go the way they used to. It might be a temporary indisposition, but after a while it becomes clear that the feeling of being leached is permanent. The teacher observes this calmly, and after extensive reflection, perhaps in conversation with a trusted colleague, comes to the conclusion that he should tell his colleagues about his doubts. He also has a good relationship to the parents, and perhaps he has asked one or two of them for advice. In short, he brings the issue to a faculty meeting, and says he has decided to stop after the 6th grade.

Perhaps the colleagues are surprised. But he is sure that he has reached the right decision. Preparations are made for a new teacher.

Whoever acts in this way, is acting out of inner strength, and may hope that, as a result of his making the right decision, a good new colleague will be found for his class. If all this happens in a timely way, we are looking at a completely justifiable procedure without any losers.

The correct appraisal of one's own situation, the well-considered personal decision, these give strength. If someone is unable to carry a class for eight years, he does not have to do so.

In fact the right decision spares the students, the parents, and the school the all-too-common phenomenon of everyone "suffering through to the bitter end".

In conclusion, one other remark. The process described here should not necessarily lead to the conclusion that this particular process ought to be generalized. It would be a distortion of pedagogy if a school were to decide fundamentally to limit the class teacher time to six years because there had been some bad experiences. For the social fabric of the school, it is appropriate that, at the beginning of 6th grade, a process of mutual pondering and consideration be implemented. Does the colleague intend to carry on into 7th and 8th grades? Does he or she want to, and is he or she able? What is the situation? Can one find the right solution for the students in open conversation?

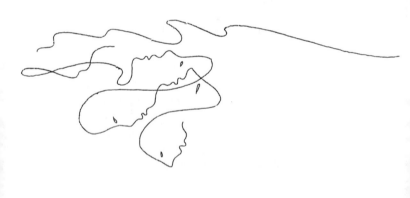

14. On Inner Preparation or Self-Education

It is not easy to speak about this topic generally. In this field especially, everything is very individual. Everyone who searches for it will find the particular path that suits him. We could leave it at that. But we can also realize that many colleagues are actually seeking access to inner preparation and yet do not find it, even though they subtly perceive an inner demand. For the true substance of a school consists in the striving of the colleagues in their inner preparation, their self-education. For that reason an attempt to portray the possibilities as broadly as possible will be ventured, in the hope that everyone will find something suitable.

If you survey the spectrum of possibilities for inner strengthening, you may well be dismayed by the endless number and variety of indications Steiner has given in this regard. From this broad spectrum, a few which may be applicable for the teacher have here been chosen.

1. Teaching is a profession which can be characterized, among other ways, by the fact that the teacher has, by definition, relationships with many people. Students, parents, colleagues: he is in active contact with

many of them each day. Most of all, of course, with the students. If you picture this wealth of encounters as a gesture, you can say: during the day the teacher lives almost entirely from inside outward. Giving, reacting, leading, indicating, instructing, arbitrating, explaining, teaching, telling.

This profession (and others similar to it) requires a self-initiated counter weight. A daily period of time must be wrung from the day's necessities. A period of time only for oneself.

This thought alone may provoke the reaction: I don't have the time for that! And then you see that having time, or not having time, is a matter of priorities: what do I, and not someone else, consider to be important?

So the question arises: can life be organized in such a way that half an hour a day can be reserved for myself? Half an hour in which nothing is scheduled. Can I organize life in such a way that there is a daily moment like that?

This is easily desired or demanded. Anyone who attempts to implement it, however, will discover that it must become the beginning of a new set of habits. For considered in this way, almost every day consists almost entirely of necessities. And should these disappear, there's the danger of falling into a hole, for suddenly nothing has to be ... The art consists of creating this "nothing needs to be" for a consciously chosen moment of the day.

2. What can you accomplish during this newly won time?

   Certainly not lesson preparation, for that is a necessity which belongs somewhere else. We had a colleague who had claimed this "time out" for himself. He used it to read five pages a day of *Theosophy*, *Knowledge of Higher Worlds* ... and *Esoteric Science* by Rudolf Steiner. And, when, after several years, he was finished, he started all over again. He didn't do more than that. But we could see that he was a carrying member of the faculty, a sort of foundation ...

3. Nowadays almost everyone has some art books on his shelves. When do you ever look into them? Perhaps you can undertake some observation of art. What would happen if I were to take some portion of my hard-won time out to study the same work of art for a week? I will learn to see; I will begin to see a lot I had not seen previously. Thoughts arise. I allow them to occupy themselves with the art work. Then one day I realize: this intensified attentiveness begins to spread into the rest of my day ...

4. Someone else enjoys contemplating on his own. He or she finds satisfaction is a concentration exercise. How long can thoughts be meaningfully devoted to a particular object without veering off? And if they do veer off, do I notice that? Or you read a poem and try to linger for a while in the experience of the beauty of the poem or its content. There are poems that are like markers around which certain thoughts and perceptions circulate. Steiner penned a large number of such

verses. But you can also find much in contemporary poetry.

5. When you look at the suggestions which Steiner provided for particular esoteric pupils, you see that they are shaped very individually. There is, however, one exception. He gave the Review of the Day to every pupil, every seeker. That leads to the conclusion that it is of high-ranking significance. Why might that be?

In the Review of the Day three challenges are laid down. First, you are challenged to become an observer of yourself. In other words, the exercise does not proceed from the point of view of the self, but from the point of view of an observer who observes the self from the outside in order to review—in reverse sequence—all that one did during the day without allowing any feelings which may have been present at the time to arise.

The second challenge in this exercise is the reversal of time: we consider ourselves and our experiences starting now and going back to the start of the day. Like a film in reverse, cause and effect will be reversed. In the usual sequence, I park the car, get out, take my bag, lock the car, go to the main entrance, climb the steps, unlock the faculty room, greet the colleagues, check my mail box, leave, go down the hall, upstairs, along the hall, and open the classroom door. Now these moments are stitched together in reverse order by the exercise: I am in the classroom, go out (in), close (open) the door, go through the hall, down the stairs (up the stairs), along the hall, close (open) the door to the faculty room, come from my mailbox … etc.

A third challenge in this exercise has to do with trying to observe completely what actually happened during the day. I really "look" at everything. Were there images I would have preferred not to see, or which I would have preferred to see differently? (One of the most famous review stories in world literature is the first of Charles Dickens' *Christmas Carols*. In this Victorian story, the main character, Scrooge, experiences, through the review, the very moment at which, when he realizes its consequence, he would have wanted to change.)

It's as if, for a brief moment, you can represent your own higher self, which can already practice on this side of the threshold what it achieves over yonder at night: the judgment of your own deeds.

The Review of the Day can be designed quite individually. You can try to grasp the whole day in large steps, or you can try to work through shorter, more detailed phases of part of a day. A particular focus can then also be included. (Whom did I encounter today? What did that person at the checkout line in the supermarket look like?)

6. An effective, special case of the Review of the Day, especially for pedagogues, is the exercise of presence of mind in the realm of the senses. Generally speaking, we encounter our students with our "soul antenna" on alert. Almost always, it is the child's or student's face we consider. We easily forget the rest of the appearance. For this Steiner recommends a drastic exercise: impress upon yourself how the other

looks. What kind of clothing, what kind of colors, etc. did he or she wear? In other words, pay attention to something (seemingly) unimportant, something insignificant. Can I remember that in the evening? So it's precisely not the "soul" aspect (which would be easy to remember, especially the facial expression) but rather something we usually don't take into account.

This exercise is difficult. It requires (or develops) a most unusual presence of self in the senses. However, once this is achieved, your engagement with the day changes. You discover that you were a dreamer, and you start, step by step, to wake up. This wakefulness then turns out to be a remedy for the fatigue caused by the daily flood of sense impressions.

7. Steiner gave the teachers three groups of attitudes, or virtues, which may be considered, attempted, and practiced. What does "practice" mean in this case? It means that we occupy ourselves with something to such an extent that we begin to embody it and it becomes part of our (acquired) character. All the following exercises include mighty perspectives. These cannot all be included here. But in the time out you create for yourself, they should be taken into account again and again.

The first group of attitudes is simple and at the same time all inclusive. The night before his first lecture on *Study of Man*, Steiner exhorts the future teachers to consider that the form of the school, about to be realized, is one into which "everyone must carry, that which gives each of us the full responsibility for what we have to do. Everyone must be fully responsible."

The sentence points at the "we" and the individual responsibility. Then, on the same occasion, the point is made that everything should be carried out in such a way that the school is unified, that integration ensues. What does this mean? Probably not unification in contrast to differentiation or individualization. Rather, unification in the sense of endowing identity. This, then, exists only partially in the (traditional) forms, but very strongly in those which the teachers are about to create. (This "identity-endowing" activity alludes to *Study of Man*, the "preparatory course". Naturally, such unification, or identity, has to be re-created ever and again.)

The second group consists of the seven Teachers' Virtues which Steiner introduced to the teachers at the end of the preparatory course: three at the end of the 14th lecture of *Study of Man*; four after the final meeting to determine the schedule (*Practical Advice to Teachers*, GA 294, Stuttgart, September 6, 1919). It's best to quote them exactly:

1. Imbue yourself with the power of imagination
2. Have courage for the truth
3. Sharpen your feeling for responsibility of soul
4. The teacher should be a person of initiative in large things as in small things
5. The teacher should be a person who is interested in everything worldly and human

6. The teacher should be someone who, inwardly, never compromises with untruth
7. The teacher must not dry up or get sour.

The first three attitudes, or virtues (they could also be competencies) can be clearly distinguished from the subsequent four. In the latter, you can easily recognize the stamp of the temperaments. Here the temperaments have transformed their shadow side into capacities. So, for example, the choleric has changed from being a tyrant into being a person of initiative. Such a "purified" temperament can be acquired by anyone. The sanguine has changed himself from a person of chaos into a person of deep interest in everything human and worldly. This characteristic is also available to anyone. So, too, the phlegmatic, who attains the strength of endurance, of loyalty (uncompromising), and the melancholic, who rejects self-reflecting sourness and seeks equanimity and good humor. The first three virtues belong to quite a different realm. They are not "physical" like the last four. They are characteristics which seem to be illumined by something higher. Where, for example, does responsibility "live"? Or (love for) Truth? Doesn't imagination also encompass the kind of thinking which must learn to include the path of living thinking? We will not be off the mark if we seek the source of these strengths there, where conscience, too, can be found.

Steiner clearly separated these virtues (competencies) into three and four. However, there is a relationship when you consider 3 and 4 as 7:

1. Imagination
2. Truth
3. Responsibility
4. Initiative
5. Interest
6. Being uncompromising
7. Not getting sour

That means:

4:         Everything begins with initiative
1 and 7: Attempt to activate the imagination, and you will not get sour
2 and 6: Attempt to activate your sense for truth, and you will not compromise with what is untrue
3 and 5: Attempt to live your responsibility; having interest will help you

Steiner characterized the third group of attitudes anew when the school was a year old. In the four lectures of *Balance in Teaching* (which he considered to be the continuation of *Study of Man*), he describes, in the second lecture, three attitudes the teacher should maintain in the presence of the individualities of the students.

- Honoring everything which has already taken place in the life of the student out of the past
- Enthusiastically pointing to the student's future
- A certain kind of protecting of that which life now "emblazons" upon the student in the present

What is our attitude toward our students' destinies? Doesn't honoring mean that everything the student carries out of the past must basically be confirmed by the teacher, because it represents the karmic will of the student? In this way, entirely new attitudes, for example toward the families, can arise.

What does enthusiastic pointing to the student's future mean? Isn't it a recognition of the student's eternal individuality, which one helps in its quest for self determination?

It is an expression for our being the place-holding ministrants until "the king has come of age".

8. The following exercise helps the self to experience itself in relationship to supersensible realms: Review the day that has just passed. Ask yourself what was successful? What not? What was my part in that? Something went really well. Was it because I was so good, or in spite of my being there? Something did not go so well, but it could have been a lot worse. There is a subtle discrepancy between my effort and the result. Steiner calls this attentiveness to the daily miracle. If you start to pay attention, you will discover to your astonishment that not a single day goes by without a small or large "miracle", in which, without your participation, progress was nevertheless achieved. That allows you to realize: somewhere, a different, superior stage-director is at work. It is the higher self, often also called angel. If we are attentive to it, our relationship to this Being, which is both independent and yet also identical with myself, will be strengthened.

9. In addition, Steiner gave the teachers two medita-

tions for their work. There is a paradox inherent here. Resolving to devote oneself to a meditative life is an entirely free deed. No one else and nothing else can prescribe that for me. Not even my belonging to a profession. But from within that profession, I can decide to add meditation to my professional practices.

These meditations for my work do not make me a better teacher, but they make me a different person. And that person can also try to be a better teacher.

To elucidate this situation, I would like to quote at length from two texts. The first quotation comes from the pedagogical lecture cycle, *The Spiritual Ground of Education*, lectures held in Oxford in 1922. They formed part of an international conference (of some 20 countries) under the auspices of the British Minister of Education, Mr. Fisher. A special lecture by Steiner, which was not included in the printed program, was announced for the first Sunday. This special lecture dealt with "Research into the Supersensible World". Regarding meditation, it says:

"We should not have any 'mystical' ideas in connection with meditation, nor indeed imagine that it is an easy thing. Meditation must be an act of complete mental clarity in the modern sense of the word. Patience and inner energy of soul are necessary for it, and above all, it is connected with an act that no man can do for another, namely to make an inner resolve and then hold to it. Once a human being resolves to meditate, that human being is performing the only completely free act there is

in human life. Within us there is always the tendency to freedom and we have, moreover, achieved a large measure of freedom. But if we think about it, we shall find that we are dependent upon heredity, upon education and upon our present life. Ask yourselves how capable you are of suddenly abandoning all you have been given by heredity, education and life in general. If we abandoned all this we would be faced with a void. But suppose we undertake to meditate regularly, in the morning and evening, in order to learn by degrees to look into the supersensible world. That is something which we can, if we like, leave undone any day. Nothing prevents it. And, as a matter of fact, experience teachers that the greater number of those who enter upon the life of meditation with splendid resolutions abandon it again very soon. We have complete freedom, for meditation is in its very essence a free act. But if we can remain true to ourselves, if we make an inner promise—not to another but to ourselves—to remain steadfast in our resolve to meditate, then this in itself will become a great and mighty force in the soul. Having said this, I want to speak of meditation in its simplest forms. Today, as I have said, I can only deal with the principles.

The following is essential. The consciousness must be focused on a central idea or combination of ideas. The particular content of the idea or ideas is not the point, but in any case it must be something that does not represent any actual reminiscences or memories. That is why it is good not to take the substance of a meditation from our own store of memories but to let another, one who is experienced in such things, give the meditation.

Not of course because he has any desire to exercise 'suggestion' but because in this way we may be sure that the substance of the meditation is something entirely new for us. It is equally good to take some ancient book which we know we have never read before, and find in it some passage for meditation. The point is that the passage shall not have been drawn from the sub-conscious or unconscious region of our own being, which are so apt to influence us. We cannot be sure about anything from these regions because it will be colored by all kinds of elements left over from our life of perception and feeling. The subject of meditation must be as clear and pure as a mathematical formula.

Take this sentence as a simple example: "Wisdom lives in the light." At the outset, one cannot set about testing this as to its truth. It is a picture. But we are not to concern ourselves with the intellectual content of the words – we must contemplate them inwardly, in the soul, letting our consciousness brood upon them. At the beginning, this will only be possible for very short periods, but they will become longer and longer. What is the next stage? We must gather together our whole life of soul in order to concentrate all the forces of thinking and perception within us upon the content of the meditation. Just as the muscles of the arm grow strong if we use them for work, so are the forces of the soul strengthened by being constantly directed to the same content, which should be the subject of meditation for many months, perhaps years. The forces of the soul must be strengthened and invigorated before real investigation in the supersensible world can be undertaken.

If practice is continued in this way, there comes a red-letter day when we become aware of an activity of soul that is entirely independent of the body. We realize too, that whereas our thinking and sentient life were formerly dependent on the body—ideation on the system of nerves and senses, feeling on the circulatory system and so on—we are now involved in an activity of soul-and-spirit that is absolutely free from any bodily influence."

The second quotation comes from the aphoristic text, *The Thresholds of the Spiritual World* (GA 17). It includes a very terse characterization of how to meditate. A step-by-step process for meditation can be found there, which in its directness is easy to follow: First, have the thought; then, enter into this thought repeatedly. You become one with it; this enables you to feel a strengthening of your soul, and connected to that, a sense of being in touch with the spiritual world. Finally, you feel a raying out of the meditation, as strength, into daily life.

The meditation which is offered here is: "I feel myself to be one in thought with the stream of cosmic events."

"The right way in which to meditate may be learned from what has just been pointed out. We first work our way through to a thought which may be realized with the means that lie ready to hand in ordinary life and knowledge. Then we submerge into that thought again and again, and make ourselves completely one with it. The strengthening of the soul is the result of living with a thought which has thus been recognized. In this case

the above thought was chosen as an example derived from the very nature of thinking. It was chosen as an example because it is very specially fruitful for meditation. But what has been said here holds good, with regard to meditation, for every thought acquired in the way that has been described. It is especially fruitful for meditation when we know the state of soul that results from the above mentioned rhythmic swing in the life of the soul. By that means we arrive in the surest way at the feeling of having been in direct touch with the spiritual world during meditation. And this feeling is a sound result of meditation. The force of it should give strength to the rest of our daily life, and in such a way that an ever-present impression of the meditative state is there the whole time, but so that one feels that from the meditative experience strength is flowing into our whole life. If the state brought about by meditation extends through daily life as an ever-present impression, it diffuses something which disturbs the mental ease of life. And the state of meditation itself will not then be sufficiently pure and strong. Meditation gives the best results when through its own character it is kept apart from ordinary life. It influences life in the best way when it is felt to be something distinct from and raised above ordinary life."

The word "meditation" is common currency, but the concept is often used incorrectly. That causes the word to be used frequently. Of course, this is an area which can be talked about only with much restraint. If one considers the two texts, one will be struck by the matter-of-factness with which Steiner talks about meditation: here a dispassionate, factual spirituality shows itself.

It is important to point this out, because it is all too easy to fall into just the opposite: a veiled, secretive muddling around with "meaningful" allusions cast in a pseudo-religious mood.

That would be inimical to life in a school, and does not express anthroposophical community building. For what is anthroposophy? It is a path. A path which wants to make the spiritual on earth effective. A concrete, sober task, which demands healthy common sense and presence of mind.

APPENDIX

Survey of the Given Exercises and their Sources

Education is self-education in two ways. Through his
or her own path of self-education, the teacher becomes
"interesting" for the students. Will they find the "environment" through their teachers, by mean of which
they can develop themselves? Isn't that the basic concept
underlying "education"?

Rudolf Steiner once called *How to Know Higher
Worlds* (GA 10) the "Educational Book" for our time.
Many of the exercises and attitudes described in the
preceding chapters originate in that book. In what follows, they are arranged according to the chapter in
which they appear here.

1. *The School Building, or the Art of Attentiveness*
   For schooling attention, for being awake in everyday
   life, the strength necessary for inner schooling can be
   found in the second condition of esoteric training. It
   states: "Feel yourself to be a part of the whole of life."
   Once you have made this attitude your own, you will
   realize more and more that you can feel yourself responsible for even the smallest things. (*How to Know*

Higher Worlds, GA 10, chapter 5, "Conditions" or "Requirements")

2. *The Classroom, or the Mirror of Habits*
   Part of self-education requires that you learn to see yourself as others see you. You observe your own thoughts, feelings, and actions. These you then look at as if from outside of yourself. Similarly, you also become aware of the surroundings, in which your thoughts, feelings, and actions are revealed. (*How to Know Higher Worlds*, GA 10, chapter 1, "Inner Peace")

3. *Colleagues, or the Virtue of Recognition*
   Contempt, antipathy, undervaluing what is commendable in the other, negative judgment, and criticism all weaken the one who is perpetrating these. Loving engagement with the merits of the other and reverence for the abilities of the other strengthen the one practicing these. (*How to Know Higher Worlds*, GA 10, chapter 1)

4. *The Colleagues at the Faculty Meeting, or the Art of Listening*
   Steiner introduced the contents of the lecture cycle *Study of Man* with a meditation in the form of an Imagination. Engaging with this Imagination strengthens the capacity for collegiality. (*Study of Man*, GA 293, Lecture 1, also available in *Toward the Deepening of Waldorf Education,* Publication of the Pedagogical Section, 2004)

5. *The School's Parents, or the Art of Being Interested in Everything that is Going On in the World*
"Secondly, my dear friends, we as teachers must be interested in everything that is going on in the world and in all that concerns mankind. All that is happening in the outside world and in the life of men must arouse our interest. If we as teachers were to shut ourselves off from anything that might interest human beings, it would be a deplorable thing. We should take an interest in the affairs of the outside world, and we should also be able to enter into all the concerns, great or small, of every individual child in our care. [...] The teacher should be one who is interested in the being of the whole world and of humanity." (*Discussions with Teachers*, GA 295, Closing Words)

6. *The Students, or the Art of Feeling Yourself a Part of All of Life*
The second condition for the path of self-education (*How to Know Higher Worlds*, GA 10, chapter 5)
The first condition discusses the necessity of striving for physical and spiritual health. Pleasure as means to an end is described, as well as how we can overcome the weaknesses that limit our effectiveness.

7. *Preparation for Teaching: Thoughts, Feelings, Actions*
See chapter 6 above. The third condition deals with acquiring the conviction that thoughts and feelings are realities, just as are actions. That gives rise to the

"world meaning" of what we experience inwardly, as opposed to a "private" reality. (*How to Know Higher Worlds*, GA 10, chapter 5)

8. *Concerning Primary Sources, or the Virtue of Veneration*
"A particular prevailing mood of soul must be the beginning. Spiritual researchers call this basic attitude the path of reverence, of devotion to truth and knowledge." *(How to Know Higher Worlds,* GA 10, chapter 1)

9. *The Lesson, or Gratitude for Life*
In many aspects of self-schooling, gratitude for life and all that we experience plays a central role. For example, see the 6th lecture (April 20, 1923, Dornach) of *The Child's Changing Consciousness and Waldorf Education* (GA 306) where we hear about the three basic virtues of gratitude, love and duty.
These virtues are represented as if the teacher's own attitude is transferred to the students and the class. Imponderables of the greatest significance are at work between the teacher and the students. This is something Steiner always kept in sight. Already at the faculty meeting of September 26, 1919 (the school had been in session for just ten days) he took note after having visited the classes, that: "The vital thing is that there is always contact, and that teachers and pupils form a unity. On the whole it is very wonderfully the case in nearly every class. I am very happy about that." (*Rudolf Steiner's Conferences*

with the Teachers of the Waldorf School in Stuttgart, vol. 1. GA 300a)

Following this remark, Steiner points out that it is necessary for the teachers, too, to strive to build such a unity with each other and with the spiritual world.

10. Something About Child Study

This way of working—having the faculty concern itself with the hardships of a student—demands great competence in the realm of inner self-regulation. A few questions will be listed: how objective can my portrayal be? How inwardly free is my contribution (or am I driven because I like to hear myself speak)? How inwardly pure, free of preconceptions, can my listening be? Could I perhaps wait with my contribution? Do I inwardly find the right moment for my contribution? If I only listen, can I still be inwardly completely active, completely engaged, or is there a risk of "shutting off"? (Meaning, though physically present, inwardly I've already checked out.)

Now the remarkable fact is that the success of a child study depends, in good measure, on such subtleties. These are subtleties, which can, however, intensify the study enormously.

To this end all that is developed by the so-called "basic" or "subsidiary" exercises is needed. Steiner describes these in various ways, in relation to self-education. (*Occult Science*, GA 13; *Theosophy*, GA 9; *How to Know Higher Worlds*, GA 10)

For the sake of orientation, the sequence, taken from the last of the above-mentioned texts, follows:

Control of thought
Control of will
Equanimity
Positivity
Openness
Equilibrium

Needless to say, the impression that these exercises are relevant only for child study is not accurate. All that is portrayed in these descriptions works on the entire human being. The stronger the "generally human" capacities, the better will be the unfolding of the professional life.

11. *Forces of Health in the Life with the Children and Students, or How we Find Active Equanimity*

In Steiner's day, i.e. at the beginning of the 20th century, it was most unusual, even dreadful and outrageous, to talk or write publicly about what we today call "inner self-rule" or "self-education". To deal with public consciousness, Steiner had to break the accumulated ice of hundreds of years, ice that the world divided into belief and knowledge. Ice which kept thinking under control, and which punished any flouting of these boundaries with dismissal: "What you think is nonsense. Such thoughts make you socially unacceptable" and so on. Later generations will honor Steiner's deed of having offered a "self-educating book" like *How to Know Higher Worlds* to the public in 1909.

This book contains a description of the conditions

required for self-schooling or self-education. They are all qualities that can be applied in daily life. In as much as one's life with the students is also a part of this daily life, these conditions can also unfold their healing effectiveness there, once they are taken up by the soul.

Already the first condition touches on a grave factual complexity. This is the question of energy, the question of how we remain healthy in life (and therefore also in our pedagogical profession). The theme of the first condition is spiritual and physical health. What is the relationship of "pleasure" to duty? How do we balance responsibilities with our own health, to protect ourselves from becoming exhausted?

The suggestion is: work inwardly with the original indications. Following, just to provide an initial orientation, are the seven themes:

1. Keep in view the need to promote bodily and spiritual health.

2. Consider yourself to be a part of the whole of life. Much is contained in the fulfillment of this condition.

3. It is necessary to raise yourself to the understanding that thoughts and feelings have as much significance for the world as actions.

4. The true human being does not abide in the "outer" but in the inner realm.

5. Steadfastness must follow a decision once it is made.

6. Develop the feeling of gratitude toward all that comes toward you in life.

7. All of the six conditions enumerated above must be unified in a seventh: to tirelessly meet life in the way these conditions demand.

12. *Punishment or the Opportunity for Originality*
Research into the theme of "resilience" elucidates the meaning of positive school-time memories. All teaching is a sowing. And the seeds will sprout. If we punish, that too will sprout. Gratitude, joy, positivity toward life, these come from reminders that "punishing" what was punishable may be able to modify it to become something future bearing, healing. A direction for proper treatment in this realm is contained in the last two chapters. Finding the properly calibrated punishment can be the result of our own school time and childhood. What happened to me? How does it live in my soul? How might it have been different? Often we teachers find ourselves in situations in which the correction takes place entirely verbally. The third exercise of the so-called eight-fold path focuses our attention on the "what" and the "how" of talking. Is what I am saying truly an expression of my being—as I want it to be—or do unnoticed automatic habits, which "make me talk", creep in? (*How to Know Higher Worlds*, GA 10, chapter 6, "Some Results of Initiation")

Glossary

Abitur: a final examination at the end of high school that, if passed, makes possible access to universities. These examinations take place in France, Holland, Germany, Austria, and other European countries. In the U.K. the equivalent exams are called "A levels".

Astral body: the soul, characterized by inner sentience and feeling; the seat of wish, want, desire, highest yearnings and deepest urges.

Ego: the Identity of the human being, the Self; sometimes also translated as the "I".

Etheric body: that aspect of the human being (also of plants and animals) that constitutes the energetic flow of formative life forces. They are responsible for regulating health and daily life-activities such as like intelligence, memory, automatic processes (habits), and the execution of basic life skills.

Eurythmy: a new art of movement through which music and word become visible. More than simply making visible the sounds of music and speech, every gesture is an expression of a soul quality.

Rückschau: a daily review of the day in reverse order. In this exercise, you look back on the day just passed from the perspective of an objective onlooker, another person looking on yourself from the outside. You see the images of the day as in a movie running backwards, and you observe yourself and what happened during the course of the day — but with no trace of judgment.

Sheath: in anthroposophy this term is used to identify the principle layers that surround the Identity or Ego of the human being. They can be imagined as residing "within" the human body and surrounding the inner core, or Identity, or be imagined as residing "without" and surrounding the body. From the first perspective (working from the inside out): surrounding the Self, or Identity, is the Astral Body or Soul Configuration. Around that, but in close connection to it, is the Etheric Body (also called the Life Body, or Body of Formative Forces).

Christof Wiechert

«Solving the Riddle of the Child»
The Art of Child Study

It may be a truism to say that every teacher should make efforts to understand his pupils. Our real understanding, after all, can be a sure foundation and support for children's whole development; and without this our lessons will be a random undertaking that connects with our pupils, at best, in a superficial way only. A skilled teacher seeks to understand his pupils so that he can raise learning beyond mere compulsion or drill. It was Rudolf Steiner's ideal that the weekly pedagogical meetings in Waldorf schools should support teachers' continually developing insight into their pupils. He exhorted them to 'become psychologists' but did not mean this in the commonly understood sense. He himself demonstrated this 'art of evolving insight' in the faculty meetings in which he participated on many occasions. One can say that it is an essential part of the quality of our work as teachers for us to develop these skills of perception, reflection and insight. Christof Wiechert here picks up these suggestions of Steiner's anew. He elaborates from them the art of the child study as a key tool in nurturing pupils development and, at the same time, teachers' own growing powers of insight. In short the approach described here can enliven the educational and social dimensions of a whole school community.

224 p., Pb., ISBN 978-3-7235-1527-3

Verlag am Goetheanum